ISSUES IN SOCIOLOGY
Edited by Robert G. Burgess

Research Methods

Robert G. Burgess

*Professor of Sociology and Director of the Centre
for Educational Development,
Appraisal and Research
University of Warwick*

Nelson

Thomas Nelson and Sons Ltd
Nelson House Mayfield Road
Walton-on-Thames Surrey
KT12 5PL UK

51 York Place
Edinburgh
EH1 3JD UK

Thomas Nelson (Hong Kong) Ltd
Toppan Building 10/F
22A Westlands Road
Quarry Bay Hong Kong

Thomas Nelson Australia
102 Dodds Street
South Melbourne
Victoria 3205 Australia

Nelson Canada
1120 Birchmount Road
Scarborough Ontario
MIK 5G4 Canada

© Robert G. Burgess 1993

Published by Thomas Nelson and Sons Ltd 1993

ISBN 0-17-438 463-7
NPN 9 8 7 6 5 4 3 2 1

Printed in Hong Kong.

Contents

Acknowledgements

The author and publishers wish to thank the following who have kindly given permission for the use of copyright material:

Blackwell Publishers for extracts from 'Evidence and Proof in Documentary Research' by J. Platt, *Sociological Review*, Vol. 29, No. 1, 1981 and 'The Research Ethics of Pseudo-Patient Studies' by M. Bulmer, *Sociological Review,* Vol. 30, No. 4, 1982.

The Birmingham Evening Mail, 25th August 1992.

The Birmingham Post, 25th August 1992.

Cambridge Journal of Education for an extract from *Keeping a Research Diary* by R. G. Burgess, Vol. 11, No. 1, 1981.

JAI Press Ltd for extracts from 'Becoming an Ethnomethodology User: Learning a Perspective in the Field' by S. Fox, ed R. G. Burgess, *Reflections on Field Experience*, 1990; 'Reflections on Fieldwork in Stressful Situations' by S. Cannon, ed R. G. Burgess, *Learning About Fieldwork* 1992; 'Making Sense of the Research Setting and Making the Research Setting Make Sense' by O. Parry, ed R. G. Burgess, *Learning About Fieldwork*, 1992; 'Ethnography, Personal Data and Computers' by A. V. Akeroyd, ed R. G. Burgess, *Conducting Qualitative Research*, 1988.

Longman Group UK for an extract from *Data Collection in Context* by S. Ackroyd and J. A. Hughes, 1981.

Longman Publishing Group for an extract from *Educational Research: An Introduction* by Walter R. Borg and Meredith Damien Gall (5th edition). Copyright © 1989 by Longman Publishing Group.

The Macmillan Press Ltd for extracts from *Part-Time Crime: An Ethnography of Fiddling and Pilferage* by J. Ditton, 1977 and *Methodological Issues in Social Surveys* by M. Maclean and H. Genn, 1979.

NFER (in-house) for an extract from *The Quest for Coherence* by P. Weston and E. Barrett with J. Jamison, 1992.

Oxford University Press for an extract from *The Voice of the Past* by P. Thompson (2nd edition), 1978.

Sage Publications for extracts from 'Questionnaires' by R. Newell, ed N. Gilbert, *Researching Social Life*, 1993 and 'Analysing Other Researchers' Data' by M. Procter, ed N. Gilbert, *Researching Social Life*, 1993.

Sage Publications, Inc. for extracts from *Learning From The Field* by W. F. Whyte. Copyright © 1984 by Sage Publications, Inc.; *Writing Up Qualitative Research* by H. F. Wolcott. Copyright © 1990 by Sage Publications, Inc.

M. Stacey for an extract from *Methods of Social Research*, 1969.

The Sun, 26th August 1992.

The University of Chicago Press for an extract from *Street Corner Society* by W. F. Whyte, (3rd edition), 1981.

Every effort has been made to trace all the copyright holders, but if any have been inadvertently overlooked the publishers will be pleased to make the necessary arrangement at the first opportunity.

Series Editor's Preface

The aim of the *Issues in Sociology* series is to provide easy access to debates and controversies in different fields of study within sociology. In particular, the series is designed for students who are beginning sociology as part of sixth form study or in further education, or in adult and continuing education classes.

The books in the series are written by authors who have wide experience of research and teaching in a special field of study where they have been directly involved in key debates. In this way, they are able to communicate the richness of the subject to the student. At the beginning of each volume, an introductory essay presents an outline of the field where key issues, problems and debates are identified. In subsequent chapters, the student is provided with commentaries, extracts, questions for discussion, essays and guides to further reading. The result is a work book that can be used by the individual student or by teachers working with small groups or a whole class.

Altogether the material in each volume seeks to convey the way in which sociological research involves a knowledge of theory and method as well as a detailed understanding of an area of study.

This volume on research methods introduces students to techniques of social investigation and some of the debates that surround their use. The materials have been assembled to help students conduct their own investigations and evaluate the work of others. Overall, this collection of material provides a guide to the ways in which social researchers work.

Robert G. Burgess
University of Warwick

Preface

Research is central to sociological work. Sociologists routinely evaluate research evidence as well as collect, analyse and report data in their own studies. In this respect, all sociologists require a knowledge of research methods to evaluate adequately the way in which studies have been conducted and to plan their own investigations. An understanding of the range of research methods that can be used is essential for sociologists beginning their careers in schools, further education colleges and higher education institutions as many introductory courses demand research skills. While all courses require students to evaluate evidence, many courses also give students the opportunity to design, collect, analyse and report data in a small scale study.

Students who engage in research therefore need to be acquainted with research methods. However, it is important to remember that there is no standard set of techniques of investigation which can be routinely used. Instead, the methods of investigation are surrounded by processes and problems that sociologists need to handle. Accordingly, the chapters in this book have been designed to introduce students to some of the main issues and debates concerned with the use of research methods. It is to be hoped that such an approach will equip students with a knowledge of a range of research methods, whilst sensitising them to the issues and problems that researchers need to resolve within their studies.

In preparing this book I have kept in mind the stimulus-response questions found in examination papers and also questions that need to be addressed in project work. Accordingly, the questions at the end of each chapter are designed to assist in project work rather than be the basis for conventional essay writing.

I am indebted to a range of students and teachers in schools, colleges and higher education institutions, especially students who have taken courses with me at the University of Warwick. They have all influenced the way in which I have thought about social research and the way in which research methods can be effectively communicated to the beginner. This book has therefore been designed as a contribution to the development of social research at Advanced level, on Access courses and in introductory courses devoted to research methods in higher education. In preparing this material for publication I am particularly indebted to Su Powell who has efficiently and effectively produced the manuscript. Needless to say any errors or omissions are my own.

Robert G. Burgess
University of Warwick

1 Methods of social investigation: an introduction

The last decade has witnessed considerable developments and changes in discussions of research methods. No longer are methods considered to be a standard set of techniques that can be applied to any project. In contrast, researchers have begun to discuss some of the processes and problems associated with using methods of social investigation. Accordingly, there has been a shift away from the 'ideal type' process of social research, which can be found in many 'methods' textbooks, where research is subdivided into a number of discrete steps and stages as shown in Figure 1.

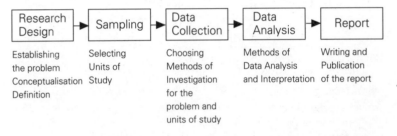

Research Design	Sampling	Data Collection	Data Analysis	Report
Establishing the problem Conceptualisation Definition	Selecting Units of Study	Choosing Methods of Investigation for the problem and units of study	Methods of Data Analysis and Interpretation	Writing and Publication of the report

(Burgess, 1985, p.6)

Figure 1 An Ideal Typical Research Process

Such an approach is based heavily on the hypothetico-deductive model that many social researchers thought natural scientists always used until accounts were published of the way in which natural scientists work. One study of particular note by James Watson (1968) entitled *The Double Helix* gave a personal account of the discovery of DNA which indicated that science seldom involves a straightforward logical sequence. Instead, it involves some guesswork, competition, rivalry and lucky breaks. It is a process of investigation which does not rely on mere technique.

Such accounts provide clues to the problems associated with the ideal typical process of social investigation which has several flaws. Firstly, it suggests that social research can be reduced to a set of discrete steps or stages. Secondly, it reduces social research to a set of technical operations. Thirdly, it assumes that each stage leads on to the next and overlooks the ways in which principles of design and sampling have to be considered at the time of writing up a report, just as issues concerned with dissemination and publication need to be thought about when a project is designed. Fourthly, data collection and data analysis are not isolated but inform each other during the course of an investigation. Fifthly, the way in which theory is used and developed within a research project is omitted from such a model as is the social, ethical and political problems that surround the research process.

Accordingly, researchers have shifted away from accounts of research as a neat sequence of procedures towards discussions of research as a process in which methods of social research are considered *alongside* the social, ethical and political problems associated with the conduct of social investigation. In this respect, research methods are not seen as standard techniques but are part of a process that links to the research problem, the researcher and the process of research. This approach to research methods emphasises the ways in which methods are modified to deal with particular situations and as such are a matter for discussion and debate. A key problem for any researcher to address is how to select methods of research: an issue to which we now turn.

☐ Choosing Methods of Social Investigation

There is no 'best' method of conducting social research. Instead, researchers need to consider the kind of research question they wish to pose and the most appropriate methods of research and techniques of data collection. A summary of some of the main choices that are available for the social researcher is shown in Figure 2.

As Figure 2 indicates, there is a range of different styles of investigation using experiments, surveys and case studies (such as ethnography) and to this can be added historical research which would include documentary evidence, oral histories and visual evidence. For the researcher a choice has to be made depending on the research problem.

If an investigation is about the effect of a particular reading scheme in a primary school, a researcher might set up an experiment with two groups of children, one of which used the scheme

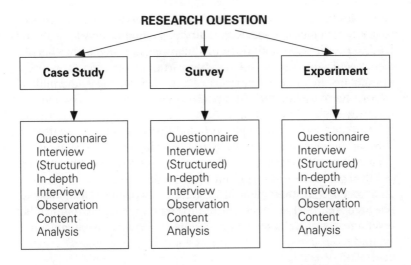

(de Vaus, 1986, p.6)

Figure 2 A Range of Methods of Research and Techniques of Data Collection

and the other which did not, to see the effects of the scheme on pupils' reading. Clearly, such an approach is very complex as the researcher has to be sure that the experiment is established in such a way that the effect of the reading scheme is measured. In addition, ethical issues need to be addressed about whether such experiments should be conducted.

Meanwhile, if a researcher wants to find out what reading schemes are used in all primary schools in different parts of the country it is most appropriate to use a survey. In this case, contacting all primary schools in England and Wales is most effectively done by means of a postal survey using a questionnaire. However, researchers would need to consider who should receive the questionnaire: the teacher responsible for reading, a class teacher, or a headteacher. No matter what decision is taken, not all the problems associated with questionnaires will be resolved, but the researcher needs to consider what will produce the highest response rate and the most accurate responses.

Finally, if a researcher wished to examine the social processes associated with the use of reading schemes and books in a primary school, it would be appropriate to conduct a case study based on ethnographic methods. This would allow the researcher to observe the way in which teachers and pupils used books and reading schemes. In addition, interviews could be conducted with teachers and pupils and documents on reading, books, the library and resources could be collected as part of this project. The result would be an in-depth portrait of one school, but the problem would be the inability of the researcher to generalise beyond the one school.

Any study will have limitations and therefore many researchers attempt to eliminate these problems by using different methods of investigation. However, there not only needs to be a consideration of the methods to be used, but also the time available to conduct the study and the financial resources available. Nevertheless, researchers need to consider the different approaches that can be taken to a research problem to produce data that are reliable and valid.

☐ Combining Methods of Social Investigation

While it is important for researchers to consider the appropriateness of particular research methods for the research problem posed, it is also essential to consider the ways in which methods can be used to complement each other in order to obtain different types of information in relation to the research problem. Among the questions that need to be considered are: what kinds of methods of investigation are appropriate for the research problem? What kind of information can be used that is relevant to the research problem? How can the methods of investigation be evaluated? Zelditch (1962) has suggested how these questions can be addressed by examining the type of information required in relation to the methods of investigation available. The results are summarised in Table 1.

This summary illustrates that the researcher cannot obtain different kinds of information using the same methods. However, some investigators have gone further and argued that methods need to be considered for the ways in which they can be integrated. Indeed, there are many studies that draw on different kinds of data. However, we still need to consider whether the researcher has just used different methods or integrated their methods, their theories and their data. Furthermore, it is important to consider how different methods may be used to focus on the same unit of study or to examine different aspects of the same study. Often

Table 1   Types of information and methods of obtaining it

Information types	METHODS OF OBTAINING INFORMATION		
	Enumerations and samples	Participant observation	Interviewing informants
Frequency distributions	Prototype and best form	Usually inadequate and inefficient	Often, but not always inadequate; if adequate, it is efficient
Incident histories	Not adequate by itself; not efficient	Prototype and best form	Adequate with precautions efficient
Institutionalized norms and statuses	Adequate, but inefficient	Adequate, but inefficient except for unverbalised forms	Most efficient and hence best method

(Zelditch, 1962, p. 576)

when different approaches are used it is possible to cross-check data obtained from surveys and from ethnographic studies. In this respect, researchers can begin to get an advantage from using different methods of investigation. But we might ask: what is the relationship between the research problem, theories and methods of investigation?

☐ The Logic of the Research Process

Once a researcher identifies a research problem it needs to be converted into a research design where it is linked to theory. But how is this link to be made? Some sociologists have suggested a staircase model to develop survey methods which can be summarised as:

1 Formulate a research problem
2 Specify the main components as concepts
3 Hypotheses are developed
4 A sample is drawn
5 Concepts are operationalised through indicators
6 Data are collected and coded in relation to the concepts
7 The hypotheses are tested on the sample
8 The conclusion is drawn.

However, this model is problematic if we start with a problem and move towards a conclusion. A reaction against this was the idea of research as a seamless web (Mann, 1981) as shown in Figure 3.

In this model there is no beginning or end and there is no clear order as theory, observation and techniques are brought together. But the difficulty with this model is that it suggests that research methods are unproblematic.

However, if the same *logic* applies to all techniques of research then the same questions need to be addressed:

- What is the research problem?
- How can the problem be formulated?
- What could constitute proof/refutation?
- What evidence can be gathered?
- How can the data be coded?
- How do data codes match the concepts used?

(cf Mann, 1981)

In short, critical questions need to be posed when conducting research projects and evaluating published work in order to understand the place of research methods in the conduct of social

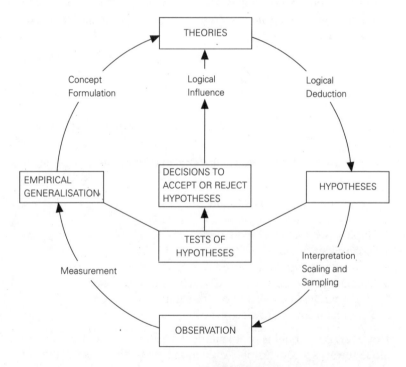

(Adaptation of Wallace, 1971, p.18)

Figure 3 'The Seamless Web' Model of the Research Process

research. It is this stance that is taken in the chapters that follow so that research methods are critically examined in terms of their use in sociological research.

Further Reading (photo copy) ↓

There are now numerous texts and collections of readings for those interested in research methods. Some key texts include:

J. Bell, *Doing Your Research Project* (Open University Press, 1987), is a guide to the conduct of research which is useful, for the beginner.

M. Bulmer (ed), *Sociological Research Methods* (Macmillan, 1984; 2nd Edition), provides a guide to the major types of sociological methods.

R.G. Burgess (ed), *Field Research: A Sourcebook and Field Manual* (Allen and Unwin, 1982), is a collection of papers on field research or ethnographic method in social research.

N. Gilbert (ed), *Researching Social Life* (Sage, 1993), provides an account of a range of methods of social research.

P. McNeill, *Research Methods* (Routledge, 1990; 2nd Edition), is a brief but readable introductory guide.

Students should also examine some first person accounts of the research process in:

C. Bell and H. Newby (eds), *Doing Sociological Research* (Allen and Unwin, 1977).

R.G. Burgess (ed), *The Research Process in Educational Settings: Ten Case Studies* (Falmer Press, 1984).

G. Walford (ed), *Doing Educational Research* (Routledge, 1991).

2 | The process of social research

Anyone who embarks upon social research quickly finds that it is much more than a matter of technique. While all researchers need to have a good understanding of research methods, they also need to have a good understanding of the process of research, that is the key elements and major phases of social investigation. The process of social research is, therefore, concerned with the way in which research projects are conceived, planned, designed, conceptualised, managed, funded, conducted, analysed and reported. In this respect, methods of investigation articulate with all these aspects of social research and will influence and be influenced by the reality of the project in which they are used.

Many researchers now produce autobiographical accounts of the processes and procedures associated with the projects on which they work. Often these accounts are written up after the project is over and as a consequence provide a reconstruction of those activities the researcher is prepared to make public to other investigators. In this respect, such accounts may overcome abstract discussions of research methods but rarely 'tell all' about the conduct of research. Instead, they are selective reconstructions of the actions and activities associated with a research project.

Some researchers who have edited collections of autobiographical accounts have attempted to assist their contributors by providing a list of the topics, themes or questions to be covered when writing about the research process. A list that I have used for this purpose is as follows:

1 What were the aims of the project?

2 What were the research aims and objectives? What key questions were addressed? How were they developed? When were they developed? Why were they developed?

3 What form did research design take? What are the technical procedures modified by research practice?

4 How was the access obtained? Who were the sponsors? What were your relationships with sponsors and gatekeepers? How did these relationships influence data collection and analysis?

5 What sampling procedures were adopted? How were they used? Why were they used? How were sampling procedures modified?

6 What major groups and events were studied? Who were the main informants? How were they selected? What was their role in the project?

7 What methods of social investigation were used? Methods of observation, participant observation, conversations, informal interviews, documentary methods, unobtrusive measures. What relationships existed between the methods? How were the methods modified in relation to the project?

8 What form did field relations take? What roles were taken in the project? What were your relationships with the informants? What was the influence of sex and gender on field relations? In the case of research teams, what were the relationships among team members? What were the power relations on the project?

9 What language skills were required in data collection and data analysis? What linguistic skills were developed in the field and how important was this for field relations?

10 What data recording procedures were used? What methods were used for recording, organising and filing field notes and keeping field diaries?

11 What was the relationship between data collection and data analysis? What were the informal processes involved in data analysis? What technical procedures were used for analysing field data? What form did the writing up take?

12 What was the role of theory in the project? What was the relationship between theory, data collection and data analysis? What form did theorising take?

13 What ethical problems were confronted in the project? How were these problems handled?

14 What form did data dissemination take? What was the impact of the project on sociology, educational studies, policy and practice and so on?

15 In what ways would you develop further projects in this area? What methodological advice would you offer?

(Burgess, 1992, pp. x–xi)

The list is not exhaustive, nor is any researcher expected to refer to every issue when writing about the research process. Instead, researchers can begin to explore their research methodology and explain what they have learned about the use of a particular research technique. However, it is important to appreciate that a major research instrument in any project is the researcher. Accordingly, many accounts of the research process deal with the biographical details of the researcher and the researcher's personal experience as it relates to the project. For example, personal as well as academic experience can influence the choice of research topic, the selection of a research site and the process of gaining access. Personal accounts also highlight the dynamic interplay between the researcher, the research design, data collection and analysis as well as theorising and writing.

Accounts of the research process indicate that social research is not static, but a dynamic process in which the researcher continually moves back and forth between the conceptual and the empirical world. It clearly demonstrates that social researchers require a range of skills: conceptual, technical and personal in order to handle the research process effectively.

☐ The Researcher and Research

One tradition of writing within the field of research methods is autobiographical, or first person accounts, where investigators are encouraged to reflect on the reasons why they engaged in particular studies. In this reading, Stephen Fox reflects on personal influences upon his work.

Reading 1

However, long before writing the May 1984 proposal I had already chosen my "research problem" in a broad way and my preferred methods. My interest in management education stemmed from my own experience as an undergraduate in business studies. I had taken an H.N.D. and a B.A. in business studies at a polytechnic where practical emphasis was supposedly emphasized. However, I had been somewhat skeptical about the practical value of much that was taught, on two main counts. In the first place, my father had started a small business, in partnership, when I was eight years old. We moved to raise the capital via a second mortgage.

When I was sixteen he folded up the business and worked as a sales representative for a year before beginning a second, this time solo, enterprise operating from home, which he gradually built up. From the start he brought his work home with him and my family life was structured around the business and its substantive concerns permeated the discussion between my parents. I was taken to his premises as a boy and learned several productive processes as well as the need to keep books and manage a small unionized labor force, other directors and customers. In many ways running a small business was part of my everyday reality before entering higher education. The difference between what I learned while doing the H.N.D. and B.A. and what seemed relevant to my father's everyday concerns seemed striking.

I was not worried personally by the difference; I happily became interested in organizational sociology and analysis and intrigued by epistemological problems, and explained the difference as a result of scale. What is taught in most business studies programs is more relevant to big organizations rather than small.

In the second place, this explanation was eroded when I went as a sandwich student to the penultimate year of my B.A. to work for a profit-center of a large nationalized corporation. I expected the managers here to be much more familiar with the terms used on my courses. But they were not. I worked in the management development and training department of the personnel function and although my main duty was co-ordinating a retrenchment and voluntary redundancy program for middle-managers, I rubbed shoulders with all the training managers and even helped them produce in-house course designs. Here they did refer to "motivation theory," "McGregor," "Herzberg," and "standard costing," but in doing so demonstrated a surprisingly low appreciation of these theories and techniques.

I returned to my final year as an undergraduate aware of the broad gap between the theories and research findings with which I was familiar and the knowledge and understanding of even senior managers in big business. In my final year, however, I found that my experience of work in industry certainly did enhance my own understanding particularly of organizational analysis and industrial relations.

As I entered business school as a Ph.D. student, I was aware of the broad gap between what the academics knew and what most practicing managers I had ever come across – from small to large business – knew. My own intellectual curiosity was firmly applied to the epistemological and methodological dilemmas of researchers particularly in organizational analysis and sociology.

Initially, I was fascinated by the topic of decision making. After a large literature review of decision making, I was more than ever *undecided* about how to go about researching the topic. However, I had a preference for using case-study methods with participant observation. My preference for the latter had again its origins in my undergraduate studies and experience of work. I had written a thesis on the basis of my work in personnel management that was a case-study of a retrenchment program. I used ethnographic methods of participant observation as well as analyzing many documents, ranging from personal letters and minutes of meetings to works newspapers and national industrial relations agreements. This was with the knowledge of my boss, the manager of training and management development, and the management association representatives with whom I came into weekly contact, although not everyone in the organization knew I was a participant observer.

S. Fox (1990), 'Becoming an Ethnomethodology User: Learning a Perspective in the Field' in R.G. Burgess (ed), *Reflections on Field Experience*, pp. 2–3.

Questions

1. List the personal influences in Stephen Fox's life which shaped his research.
2. What is the relationship between personal and academic issues in shaping Stephen Fox's work?
3. List the personal and academic issues that influence your interest in a particular field of study.

☐ Writing a Research Proposal

Having identified a field of study and an issue to investigate, researchers need to prepare a research proposal. In this reading, Lawrence Stenhouse outlines the main elements of a proposal he wrote for a project on library access and sixth-form study that was funded by the British Library.

Reading 2

The Research Proposal
When it comes to research aims, I think I have always worked with double sets of aims – one for the sponsor and one for myself! The proposal sets out the job I hope to do for the sponsor – in this case as follows:

> 1 to reconceptualize academic sixth-form education in respect to its relation to library access;

2 to draw implications for teaching in the presence of libraries and for user education;
3 to consider the significance of library access for educational opportunity at sixth-form level and draw conclusions for the organization of education and library provision at age 16–18;
4 to consider the concept and possible form of compensatory user education;
5 to document the styles of librarians and teachers as managers of knowledge;
6 to make recommendations for curriculum development in user education at sixth-form level.

The whole art of the business in funded research is to find scope for your own aims within and alongside the sponsor's aims – and without costing the sponsor anything. I saw in the project the possibility of building the theory of schooling on which I have been working for the last twenty years or so. The theme of emancipation, which I have already mentioned, is potentially a matter of conflict in the sixth form, and largely because of the growth of independent study and the student's capacity to appeal against the teacher to the library. As one of our students says in interview, teachers' encouragement of independent study places them in danger of a kind of redundancy. This is fascinating territory. So too is the possibility of making comparisons across the divide between private and state school systems. Finally, I was interested in undertaking the design and management problems of multi-site case study and hopeful of accumulating an archive through this research which would be a resource for other researches and researchers. I was confident both that I would get plenty out of the work for the British Library and that I would be able to follow my own intellectual quests, and so I was able to work in a style comfortable to my bent with comparatively little preordinate planning and plenty of responsive thinking. Look for a rich seam and then dig!

What I suppose might be called the research design is treated in the proposal under the heading, 'Method':

generalization across twenty-six descriptive case studies based upon condensed fieldwork involving tape recorded interviews, observations and collection of documents, including both qualitative and quantitative data. The fieldworkers will produce indexed case records to form an archive.

The use of the word 'generalization', here, is problematic and I must leave for later discussion: an explanation was clearly not of interest to the sponsors. The central design feature is multi-site case study based on condensed fieldwork.

L. Stenhouse (1984), 'Library Access, Library Use and User Education in Academic Sixth Forms: an autobiographical account' in R.G. Burgess (ed), *The Research Process in Educational Settings: Ten Case Studies*, pp. 213–14.

Questions

1. In what ways do Lawrence Stenhouse's research aims contribute to
   (a) theory
   (b) method
   (c) the study of libraries?
2. Describe the methods to be used in Lawrence Stenhouse's project and suggest why they may be problematic.
3. Outline the aims and objectives of a study on the use of the library in your school or college.

☐ Defining the Field

In writing a research proposal for a project, a range of issues is covered on the research problem to be studied and its relationship to theories and methods. A key element involved in writing a research proposal is the focus of the study. In this reading, Sue Cannon discusses how she defined her field of study.

Reading 3

This section is concerned with the design of the project and the choice of a methodology. As Duelli-Klein (1983, p. 38) says:

> the "what" to investigate must come prior to the decision of "how" to go about doing one's research.

My overall intention in designing the project was concerned with obtaining experiential accounts from women with breast cancer of various aspects of the disease, in other words how it *felt* to have breast cancer. The experiential element is stressed because the research was qualitative and therefore not concerned with any sort of psychological test or measurement, for example of stress or anxiety levels engendered by the illness (there is no shortage of studies which adopt these latter techniques, for example Maguire [1975], and Morris, Gear, and White [1977]).

The general objective here was to obtain the women's evaluations of, and commentaries on, their illness and its effects on their lives and relationships. Specific topics on which I wished to focus were as follows:

1 the discovery of the initial symptoms;
2 the hospital stay and diagnosis;
3 the women's feelings about their breasts;
4 in the case of those who had had mastectomies, seeing the site of the operation for the first time and using a prosthesis;
5 the women's feelings about illness in general, both in themselves and others;
6 experiences of the treatments and treatment procedures;
7 reactions of others, especially sexual partners;
8 changes in the women's lives brought about by the disease.

The choice of methodology seemed fairly self-evident. As Locker (1981, p. 17) says:

in many cases, and perhaps fortunately so, the research strategies available to a researcher are limited by the kinds of situations being studied.

It was obvious for example that survey methods and questionnaires would not yield the information I required. Similarly, there was no way of conducting the research covertly, nor had I any desire to do so. I felt that, clearly, the success of the research depended upon my being able to form relationships with the women which would involve, at the very least, gaining their confidence and trust which would, in turn, necessitate some emotional input on my part in the relationships. This point of view is clearly stated in the work of Stanley and Wise (1983, p. 162):

because the basis of all research is a relationship, this necessarily involves the presence of the researcher *as a person.* Personhood cannot be left behind, cannot be left out of the research process. And so we insist that it must be capitalised upon, it must be made full use of (emphasis in original).

Stanley and Wise go on to point out that accounts of research projects which do not consider the effects of the researcher's presence are missing out an important influence on the research itself. In the case of a project like the breast cancer study, which depended to a great extent on relationships between myself and the women, it seemed both obvious and necessary that my presence in, and involvement with, the research process would need to be written into the final account.

S. Cannon (1992), 'Reflections on Fieldwork in Stressful Situations' in R.G. Burgess (ed), *Learning About Fieldwork*, pp. 158–9.

Questions

1. How would you define Sue Cannon's field of study?
2. In what ways does her field of study link with the methods of investigation to be used?
3. Sue Cannon suggests that survey methods and questionnaires would not provide the data she required. Do you agree? Give reasons for your answer.

□ Selecting Units of Study

Having defined a field of study, researchers have to decide the units they wish to study and the ways in which they will be selected. Often there is no easy solution to this problem as Howard Newby discovered when studying farm workers.

Reading 4

I do not wish to dwell on the technicalities of sampling and questionnaire design, since they can be found in the conventional methods cookbooks, whose recipes I largely followed. As such, they are concerns which lie outside the expressed purpose of this book, *[Doing Sociological Research]*. However, some problems not customarily referred to can be highlighted briefly. Farm workers represent a highly scattered population, isolated and often socially invisible. The logistics of doing a survey are thus formidable: problems of creating a correct sampling frame, problems of contact, problems of travel, problems of interviewing as a piece of social interaction, all pile on top of each other. All sociologists believe that their own respondents present more difficulties than everyone else's, so I do not wish to overstate this; I merely wish to point out that the temptation to take some short-cuts was irresistible. In particular I sampled farms rather than farm workers, since I believed I could obtain a reliable sampling frame of farms (mistakenly, since the Ministry of Agriculture refused to co-operate and I was forced back on to the Yellow Pages) and then contact the workers via the employer. This was not only an administrative convenience, but probably also an administrative necessity. However, the result was that, in common with so many other sociological studies, I was taking the easy option of homing in on a captive set of respondents. So much sociological research takes place in an institutional setting – a factory, office, school, prison, hospital – whereby contact is made, especially with working-class respondents, via people in positions of authority over them. For despite our awareness of the 'Hawthorn effect' the practice continues, and we hope we can rectify any misconceptions of our purpose in the interview situation itself – but this in turn requires a careful and sensitive appraisal of the role required to obtain a sympathetic *rapport* with the respondent before data collection even commences.

Two important consequences follow from this. The first is that, following observations by Jack Douglas (1967) and A. V. Cicourel (1964), the method of obtaining the data is often valid sociological data in its own right. The necessity to approach farm workers via the farmer was already telling me something about the social situation of the workers I eventually interviewed: namely, that the majority *were* socially and geographically isolated, that they *were* socially invisible to many inhabitants in the locality, and that the employer *was* a significant other in their lives. In addition to this, by carefully considering the role I would need to adopt in order to obtain valid data from the agricultural workers I was to interview, I was already operating with an implicit theory of their social situation. In other words, theory and method were inseparably intertwined even at this relatively early stage in the data-collecting process. Thus the role that I quite consciously adopted was not that of researcher or investigator (which I believed ran the risk of inspiring either hostility or taciturnity), nor that of friend (which was patently inoperable), but rather that of student. I was not investigating rural society; I was studying it.

H. Newby (1977), 'In The Field: reflections on the study of Suffolk farm workers' in C. Bell and H. Newby (eds), *Doing Sociological Research*, pp. 114–15.

Questions

1. What were the difficulties in studying farm workers?
2. Howard Newby used the *Yellow Pages* for his study. Suggest the problems involved in using this approach to select farms and, in turn, farm workers.
3. How were theory and method linked together in Howard Newby's study?

☐ Establishing and Developing Field Relations

All social researchers need to establish good relationships with those with whom they work. Survey researchers and interviewers have relatively short periods of time to establish a relationship, while those engaged in observational studies can monitor the changes in their relationships over time and the way this influences the study. In this reading, Geoffrey Walford discusses the way in which his study of a City Technology College developed over time.

Reading 5

I knew that for the first few weeks I would have to be careful not to antagonize anyone, and to try to become part of the background. For the first half of term I thus wanted to adopt the standard technique of following teachers and pupils in their daily tasks. For the first few days I felt very effectively 'managed', for I was assigned to be with only 'safe' and highly trusted teachers. We were all testing the water, but as the weeks passed and I showed myself to be trustworthy, I was able to negotiate with individual teachers to watch their classes. Towards the end, there were days when I was left to fend for myself completely. All of the teachers asked agreed to allow me into their classes and most were only asked on the same day as being observed (some with only a few minutes warning).

In the classrooms I usually found myself a seat as out of the way as possible and simply watched. I took very few notes in the classrooms, but recollected at length using a tape recorder at the end of each day. I tried to describe what I had seen in each of the lessons, noting anything which struck me as being routine, unusual, or of special interest. I also noted my conversations with staff and students, and my feelings about how the research was going. Description, hunches, problems and even tentative hypotheses were all jumbled onto the innumerable tapes.

To describe what the college was doing, I had to try to understand how it was experienced by the different groups involved. To me, the most important group was the pupils (who are called students at the college). No general announcement was made to students about my presence, and I did not ask for such a statement, fearing that it might be accompanied by a demand to be always on best behaviour when I was around. Instead I relied on the student grapevine to spread the news and, in practice, it was some days before any but a tiny few knew who I was. It was four days into the study before any of the teachers in whose classrooms I was observing asked me if I would like to explain to the students what I was doing, and students did not at first ask me individually.

A problem which I had not anticipated was that both teachers and students were reasonably used to having visitors in the college, many of whom would tour the classrooms and ask both staff and students questions. These visitors might be industrialists, sponsors, governors, reporters, politicians and so on and, while teachers were usually given some warning that specific visitors would be around the college, the students generally were not. Indeed, so common were visitors that students identified them as a separate category of participants in the college and it was as if unwritten 'visitors rules' applied when they were present. Students were often told of the importance of creating a good impression for the college at all times, but especially when visitors were present. It was only after a few days that they began to realize that my own position in the college was different, and began to ask me what I was doing. I always explained that I was independent of the college, that I was writing a book about it, and that I wanted to find out what it was like for them to be there. I tried to make it clear that I would not be reporting back anything to teachers and that (generally against their wishes) no students would be named in the book. As the weeks passed, students whom I did not know would check who I was and ask me if I was really writing a book about them. The student 'bush telegraph' obviously worked, but more slowly than I expected: probably because I was simply not particularly interesting compared with the other things that were going on. A man sitting at the back of classes and asking a few questions was a poor second to the excesses of several BBC and independent television crews, or a forthcoming visit by HRH Prince Philip!

The problem with the semi-official status of 'visitor' was that I had to fight to try to indicate that I was *not* to be treated as a visitor. I was there to observe the college warts and all, and not to be the recipient of image management. This took a long time. It was four weeks before I saw more than the most minor rowdiness or misbehaviour in classrooms. Before that, the presence of a 'visitor' had been such that individuals within groups would sometimes chastise other students, by giving a look in my direction. They wanted to maintain the college's reputation if they possibly could. However, eventually, I sat in wonder as a group of boys behaved as 12 year olds do – hitting each other, moving from chair to chair, mock wrestling, and then becoming innocent and busy workers at the approach of the teacher. Again I became amazed at the ability of children convincingly to change their topic of conversation mid-sentence as a teacher comes within earshot. The teacher knew little of what was going on behind his back.

G. Walford (1991), 'Researching the City Technology College, Kingshurst' in G. Walford (ed), *Doing Educational Research*, pp. 91–3.

Questions

1. What were the key phases in Geoffrey Walford's study?
2. List the tactics that Geoffrey Walford used to establish himself in the City Technology College.
3. Consider the difficulties of establishing yourself in a new group for the purposes of study. How would you handle these difficulties?

☐ Interviewing Informants

The importance of establishing good relationships not only applies when conducting observational studies, but also when conducting interviews. Indeed, feminist researchers have highlighted the importance of the relationship when women talk to women; it is a situation that is discussed by Janet Finch in relation to studies of playgroups and clergymen's wives.

Reading 6

Both the clergymen's wives and the playgroups studies were concerned entirely with women; in both I used qualitative techniques including in-depth interviewing; and in both I talked to women in their own homes about aspects of their lives which centrally defined their identities as women – marriage, motherhood and child-rearing. My consciousness of the special character of a research situation in which women talk to another woman in an informal way, and about these issues, was heightened by reading Ann Oakley's (1981) discussion of interviewing women. Oakley takes the view that formal, survey-type interviewing is unsuited to the production of good sociological work on women. She prefers less-structured research strategies which avoid creating a hierarchical relationship between interviewer and interviewee. That sort of relationship, she argues, is inappropriate for a feminist doing research on women, because it means that we objectify our sisters.

I share Oakley's preference on both methodological and political grounds, and my own research has all been of the type which she recommends. I have also found, quite simply, that it works very well. Initially I was startled by the readiness with which women talked to me. Like every other researcher brought up on orthodox methodology textbooks, I expected to have to work at establishing something called rapport (Oakley, 1981). In my experience, such efforts are normally unnecessary when interviews are set up in the way I have described. Women are almost always enthusiastic

Book on my choice of study

about talking to a woman researcher, even if they have some initial anxieties about the purpose of the research or their own 'performance' in the interview situation. Their intentions are apparent, simply from the hospitality which one characteristically receives – an aspect of the research experience which Oakley (1981) notes is seldom mentioned in reports. In my study of clergymen's wives, I was offered tea or coffee, and sometimes meals, in all but two instances; the same happened in the majority of interviews in my playgroup study. One is, therefore, being welcomed into the interviewee's home as a guest, not merely tolerated as an inquisitor. This particular contrast was demonstrated to me in graphic form when I arrived at one interviewee's home during the playgroup study, only to find that she was already being interviewed by someone else. This seemed like the ultimate researcher's nightmare, but in the end proved very much to my advantage. The other interviewer was in fact a local authority housing visitor, who was ploughing her way through a formal questionnaire in a rather unconfident manner, using a format which required the respondent to read some questions from a card ('Do you receive any of the benefits listed on card G?', and so on). My presence during this procedure must have been rather unnerving for the housing visitor, but was most instructive for me. I recorded in my fieldnotes that the stilted and rather grudging answers which she received were in complete contrast with the relaxed discussion of some very private material which the same interviewee offered in her interview with me. My methodological preferences were certainly confirmed by this experience.

J. Finch (1984), 'It's great to have someone to talk to: ethics and politics of interviewing women' in C. Bell and H. Roberts (eds), *Social Researching*, pp. 72–3.

Questions

1. What do you consider are the special characteristics of women interviewing women for research purposes?
2. Why do you think a hierarchical relationship between interviewer and interviewee is inappropriate in feminist research?
3. Compare the characteristics of in-depth interviews and formal interviews outlined in the reading. Suggest circumstances in which each approach might be appropriate.

☐ Analysing Data

Many accounts of research and research methods focus on data collection but omit any discussion of data analysis. In this reading,

Odette Parry looks at the relationship between data collection and data analysis in a study of journalism training.

Reading 7

The process of data collection and analysis did not form distinct phases within the research process. Had I allowed this to happen, the problem of making sense of the field notes that I found at the end of the first day in the field would have multiplied one thousand fold by the end of term one. Hammersley and Atkinson (1983, p. 174) observed that in ethnography, analysis ideally starts prior to the fieldwork:

> . . . in the formulation and clarification of research problems, and continues into the process of writing up. Formally, it starts to take shape in analytical notes and memoranda; informally, it is embodied in the ethnographer's ideas, hunches and emergent concepts.

I entered the fieldwork stage of the project already one year into the research process and had accumulated a wealth of background information about journalism training. I had already begun formulating ideas and concepts I intended to test out in the field.

These early ideas were informed by a systematic appraisal of the history of British journalism training and the occupational bodies influencing its development. I had also acquired information specific to the journalism school, regarding its own particular development and about the processes of selection of students to the course. I had also interviewed three members of the teaching staff at the school.

Hence my entry into the field was accompanied by a number of embryonic ideas. These were mainly concerned with the nature of vocational training and the implications this form of occupational socialization might have for the curriculum and teaching style characteristic of the journalism school. Following the advice of Glaser and Strauss (1967) I intended to develop and ground theory in the data as an ongoing and reflexive component of the research process. Through the development of concept and category formation, the data was used to focus and reformulate my ideas as an ongoing process throughout the course of data collection. The emergent categories were then used as sensitizing devices at each point of re-entry into the field. Throughout this process I collected fieldnotes that aimed at being descriptive, analytical and self-reflective (Burgess 1984). For the purposes of retrieval and sorting of field notes, I coded in multiple categories (Lofland 1971), by indexing each occurrence of a particular type of event with an identifying letter. Events similarly indexed constituted a group or category of actions which, I felt, had something in common. In the early days of fieldwork, indexing was done on the field notes themselves, but this soon became unmanageable. At this point I switched to physical sorting. This method, used by Whyte (1955), involved making multiple copies of the field notes so the same items could, where necessary, be coded under a variety of headings.

O. Parry (1992), 'Making Sense of the Research Setting and Making the Research Setting Make Sense' in R.G. Burgess (ed), *Learning About Fieldwork*, pp. 81–2.

Questions

1. Odette Parry suggests data collection and analysis were linked in her project. What evidence supports this view?
2. What was the raw material for the data analysis?
3. Observe the events in your classroom for one hour and write descriptive, analytical and self-reflective notes about your experience. How are these notes different?

Project Questions

1. What aspects of your biography influence your research interests? Consider your personal and academic interests.
2. Outline a proposal for a small-scale project of your choice. List the aims and objectives, the research questions, methods of data collection and analysis, and plans for reporting your data.
3. Start a journal which records your reasons for selecting the topic you have chosen to investigate and the way you intend to approach the study. (This can be developed throughout your study so as to provide the raw material for an autobiographical account.)

Further Reading

C. Bell and H. Newby (eds), *Doing Sociological Research* (Allen and Unwin, 1977), is the most frequently cited set of autobiographical accounts, but very descriptive.

C. Bell and H. Roberts (eds), *Social Researching* (Routledge, 1984), contains accounts from feminist researchers.

A. Bryman (ed), *Doing Research in Organisations* (Routledge, 1988), focuses on industrial studies and provides insights into the research process.

R.G. Burgess (ed), *The Research Process in Educational Settings: Ten Case Studies* (Falmer Press, 1984), provides a discussion of research processes in relation to methods of investigation in the field of education.

R.G. Burgess (ed), *Exploring Society* (Longman, 1986) and *Investigating*

Society (Longman, 1988), both contain essays specially commissioned to discuss processes of researching twenty topic areas in sociology; they are especially suitable for 'A' level students.

P. Hammond (ed), *Sociologists at Work* (Basic Books, 1964), is a classic set of American essays which combines discussion of the conceptual and practical aspects of conducting research.

G. Walford (ed), *Doing Educational Research* (Routledge, 1991), provides discussions of different types of educational research and the research process.

3 | Principles of selection

Sampling and selection are usually associated with survey methods of social investigation. This view is far too narrow, however, as principles of selection are involved in all forms of social research. Within any investigation, the researcher needs to decide how to make a selection of the key units of study. In the literature this is discussed in terms of different kinds of sampling.

The basic distinction made in statistical sampling is between:

a probability sampling where it is possible to specify for each element of the population the probability of it being included in the sample;

b non-probability sampling where there is no way of estimating the probability of each element being included in the sample or any assurance that each element has some chance of being included.

Examples of probability and non-probability sampling are shown in the following table:

Table 1   Probability and non-probability sampling

Probability sampling	Non-probability sampling
Simple random sampling	Accidental sampling
Stratified random sampling	Quota sampling
Cluster sampling	Judgement sampling
Multi-stage sampling	Snowball sampling
Stratified cluster sampling	

Some of these forms of statistical sampling will be examined in closer detail in the readings, alongside theoretical sampling where researchers collect, code and analyse data in order to decide what to collect next. Theoretical sampling therefore encourages the researcher to address a series of questions including:
• What groups should be selected for study?
• When should these groups be observed?
• What data should be gathered?
• When should data collection end?

This approach has been advocated by Glaser and Strauss (1967) and many investigators claim to use it in their studies. However, we need to consider the differences between statistical sampling and theoretical sampling as shown in the following table:

Table 2   Theoretical sampling and statistical sampling

Theoretical sampling	Statistical sampling
1 Does not end until new concepts and categories no longer appear.	**1** Ends when a sample that was predetermined has been observed.
2 Judged by the quality of theory developed.	**2** Judged by the way it conforms to sampling theory.

Despite such differences, some sociologists such as Denzin (1970) have identified a series of principles associated with all forms of sampling which include the following:

a the importance of sampling being theoretically directed;
b the use of a sampling frame;
c the principle of samples being representative of a population;
d the use of comparisons;
e the principle of sampling being made public by the researcher.

Within social research, these principles need to be kept in mind during the course of all investigations. Yet it should also be remembered that sampling and selection occur in a project from the time a researcher chooses a specific field of study and a focus for the research design, to the time when in data analysis and writing up certain situations, time periods, events and people are selected for discussion. In short, sampling takes place throughout a research project and is not confined to a discrete phase of the investigation. In choosing between different kinds of sample, a number of criteria will be involved including: the nature of the research problem to be investigated; the availability of a sampling frame; the financial support for a project; its duration and the methods of data collection to be used. Accordingly, researchers need to be acquainted with the main forms of sampling to which we now turn.

☐ Types of Probability Sampling

In order to obtain a sample that is representative of a population, researchers need to become involved in probability or 'random' sampling where each unit of the population has a known chance of being included in the sample. There are several different types of probability sample which Alan Bryman outlines in this reading.

Reading 1

Types of probability sample

The most basic form of probability sample is the *simple random sample*. With a simple random sample, each unit in the population has an equal probability of inclusion in the sample. In order to create a simple random sample, a listing of the population, known as the *sampling frame*, is required. The sample is selected from this listing using a table of random numbers. Each unit is given a number from 1 to N, where N is the total number of units in the population. In order to select a sample of size n, a random numbers table is scrutinized until n units have been selected. Thus, if the first number in the table between 1 and N is 78, then the unit corresponding to that number will be selected, and so on until there are n units. The important point to notice with this procedure is that the human element is eliminated. If the researcher simply chose his or her respondents or relied on people being available, there is a strong chance that an unrepresentative sample would ensue, since a non-probability form of sampling would have been employed. By removing the human hand and relying on random numbers, the possibility of a systematic bias is reduced. A variation on the simple random sample is the *systematic sample*. Here the researcher samples directly from the sampling frame. Thus, if n is to be 100 and N is 1,000, implying a 1 in 10 sample, a random start of any number between 1 and 10 is made on the list, and the corresponding unit is the first to be included in the sample. Thereafter, every tenth unit is selected. If the random start indicates that the eighth unit is selected, then the eighteenth, twenty-eighth, thirty-eighth and so on will be included. Systematic sampling can only operate accurately if there is no inherent order to the listing of the population in the sampling frame. If such an order exists, there is the possibility of bias, since the structure of the sampling frame may result in the over- or under-representation of particular categories of the population.

A further type of probability sample that is often used is the *stratified random sample*. With this kind of procedure, the population is divided into strata, and simple random samples are taken from each stratum. Thus, a researcher interested in the variables with which job satisfaction among non-manual workers is associated in a firm may take the view that it is important to ensure that all functional areas within the firm are fully represented. The population of non-manual workers can then be divided into the various functional areas or strata (that is, production, marketing and sales, personnel, R & D, financial accounting and so on). By taking a simple random sample from each of these strata, the researcher can ensure that the resulting sample will accurately reflect the population in terms of functional areas. A simple random or systematic sample taken from the entire population *might* have led to an accurate representation, but the stratified random sample can enhance the likelihood of accuracy. This procedure is likely to be of particular importance when it is anticipated that the criterion on which the sample is stratified is an important characteristic that may be associated with variations in job satisfaction and the other variables of interest. Two or more stratifying criteria can be employed in conjunction. The researcher may additionally wish to stratify the population according to level (that is, upper, middle and lower management, clerical and so on). A number of combinations of functional area plus level (for example, middle management in production, sales, personnel, R & D and accounting) would ensue. Thus, five functional areas plus four levels of non-manual work would yield twenty strata from which samples would be taken. Such sampling can be either *proportionate or disproportionate.* In the former case, if we want a sample of 500 and there are 2,000 non-manual employees in the firm, a random sample of 1 in 4 would be taken from each stratum. However, if one of the functional areas is small (perhaps a small unit of only fifteen people as in an R & D group), proportionate sampling will produce an unacceptably small number from that area, especially if variations in job satisfaction are likely to be linked to categories of functional area in subsequent analysis. Accordingly, a larger proportion of persons working in R & D (or possibly all of them) will be included in the sample, and slightly lower proportions taken from the other strata. However, the decision about whether to stratify the population is bound to be affected by the extent to which the relevant data are readily to hand. If a firm has good records which allow persons in different functional areas and at various levels to be readily identified, the extraction of a stratified random sample is likely to be straightforward. If the relevant data are not readily available, the time and cost involved may make stratified random sampling prohibitively expensive. Similarly, when conducting survey research on organizations as such, if the information is available, a number of potential stratifying criteria can be envisaged. Cameron, Kim and Whetten employed this technique in their study of higher education organizations in the USA:

A stratified, random sample representative of all four-year colleges and universities in the United States was selected on the basis of size (200–20,000 FTE [full-time equivalent students]), control (public/private), enrollment and revenue change (growth, decline, stability), and degrees offered (bachelor's, master's, doctorate).

(Cameron, Kim and Whetten, 1987, p. 228)

Thus, this study employed four stratifying criteria ensuring a sample that was 'very close to the demographics of four-year institutions in the US' (p. 228).

The final type of sample worthy of mention is the *multi-stage cluster sample*. This form of sampling is likely to be of particular use when the researcher is seeking to investigate organizations which are widely dispersed. The procedure entails dividing a geographical region into constituent areas (such as states into counties in the USA or counties into boroughs in England and Wales). Counties or boroughs (that is, clusters) are then randomly sampled, and then organizations from each cluster are randomly sampled. The chief advantage of this approach is that, when interviews are to be conducted, interviewers will be more concentrated in particular areas, thereby saving much time and money on travel.

A. Bryman (1989), *Research Methods and Organisation Studies*, pp. 107–10.

Questions

1. Explain what you understand by:
   (a) a random sample
   (b) a systematic sample
   (c) a stratified random sample
   (d) a multi-stage cluster sample
2. What is a 'sampling frame'? Give examples of sampling frames that could be used in studies of schools, churches, hospitals, communities.
3. Conduct a one in ten sample of the year group in your school or college. Consider the issues raised by the sampling frame that you use.

☐ Quota Sampling

One of the ways in which researchers have attempted to approximate random sampling is through the use of quota sampling. This approach overcomes some of the difficulties associated with selecting respondents and so has advantages in terms of cost and overcoming bias. However, there are also difficulties with this approach.

Reading 2

Instead of seeking a random sample from a population in which each member has a known, calculable, and non-zero probability of inclusion, quota sampling proceeds by deliberately selecting a sample which reflects a known composition of the whole population. These days much is known about the social composition of the population thanks largely to the activity of government through the national census. It is thus possible to make sure that any sample we choose has the same distribution of characteristics as the general population. By selecting for a sample a definite 'quota' which reflects the proportion of people in the general population with the same characteristics, we have, *prima facie*, reason to think the sample representative. The criteria most commonly used to establish how many people we should have in a sample are: age, sex, marital status, and social class, although different criteria may be used in investigations as appropriate. These criteria are called 'quota controls' because they are used to limit the number of respondents chosen within the predetermined quotas.

Strictly speaking, of course, this kind of sampling does not allow statistical theory to be used to make generalisations about the whole population since the selection of cases within the quota category is not done strictly according to random sampling procedures. For this reason, it has attracted heavy criticism from statisticians and methodologists. On the other hand, quota sampling, it could be argued, is informed by sociological principles. Most importantly, the quota sampling procedure takes into account the fact that people in different social circumstances will have different views; and the sample is chosen so that more salient features and differences that are thought to exist are proportionately represented. To some extent this aim can be achieved by stratifying a random sample appropriately in the manner discussed in the previous section. But there are very often insurmountable practical difficulties in doing this. It is very difficult, for example, to stratify in advance a sampling list such as an electoral register by social class or education. Random sampling, it might be argued, makes rather few concessions to the fact that human populations are not socially well mixed: indeed, they tend, by and large, to develop a distinct homogeneity within subgroups. Quota sampling, intelligently used, can deal with these difficulties effectively.

Instead of all the difficulties of finding or developing an appropriate sampling frame, and of drawing the sample randomly from the list, the quota sample is usually drawn by the interviewer. The researcher goes out looking for respondents who conform to quota requirements, either by knocking on doors, or, sometimes, by simply asking people in the street to participate. To do this without quota controls would be extremely dangerous. To include all the people in a particular street could be to take people of rather similar income and, therefore, consumption habits. To select respondents in the High Street on a Monday, would be to include an excessive proportion of women of child-bearing age. Quotas go some way to ensuring that the researcher does not introduce such biases. By working the High Street on a Monday, the interviewer will rapidly fill the quota of married women 20–35, and possibly of men and women over 65, but he or she will probably have to look elsewhere for men of other ages and social classes. Researchers using quotas have to ask a number of preliminary questions to ensure that people encountered do fulfil quota requirements, and if they do not, politely break off the interview. There are obvious difficulties with this, of which the main ones are, firstly, that asking personal questions is not always the best way to begin an interview and so may produce a large number of refusals which may itself introduce a bias. Secondly, it is a great temptation for an interviewer to classify respondents into categories where they are most needed rather than where they really belong, especially when the job is nearly complete and respondents from particular categories seem particularly rare.

S. Ackroyd and J.A. Hughes (1981), *Data Collection in Context*, pp. 42–4.

Questions

1. What do you understand by the term 'quota sampling' and how can it be used?
2. What problems associated with random sampling are overcome by quota sampling?
3. What are the problems involved in quota sampling for the researcher?

□ Snowball Sampling

There are some populations where it is not easy to get access to a sampling frame or a random sample. In particular, this problem exists with the criminal population where a random sample of those detained by the police or those in prison would result in concentrating on the unsuccessful. Accordingly, as Martin Plant indicates, other approaches have to be used.

Reading 3

There has been a major debate about the usefulness of field research in criminology. Generally, writers have preferred to avoid field-work, justifying this on the grounds that it is too subjective and unscientific. Polsky accuses criminologists of 'copping out' or failing to come to terms with the realities of their subject. He emphasizes the fact that the official crime statistics do not represent crime in general and advocates more frequent use of field-work to look beyond the statistics. He rejects Sutherland and Cressey's assertions that to observe criminals, one must 'associate with them as one of them'. Polsky maintains that it is fully possible to collect information from criminals without joining in with the commission of their crimes.

Polsky details the problems of interacting with criminal deviants, but is emphatic that successful observation is possible. He describes the technique he uses:

'In my experience, the most feasible technique for building one's sample is *"snowballing"*: get an introduction to one criminal who will vouch for you with the others. (It is of course best to start at the top if possible, that is, with an introduction to the most prestigious person in the group you want to study.)' (Polsky 1969:129)

With regard to the ethical considerations of this approach, Polsky has this to say: 'You must draw the line between yourself and the criminal. Precisely where to draw it is a moral decision that each researcher must make for himself in each research situation' (1969:132). He adds that one must keep faith with one's informants and, of necessity, write more vaguely than one would prefer, in order to preserve anonymity.

Using the technique of 'snowballing', which has already been discussed, 200 drugtakers were interviewed during August, September, and October, 1972. Only eight people refused face-to-face to be interviewed, but I do not know how many refused indirectly when approached by other respondents.

The refusals

1) working-class male, unemployed
2) female non-manual worker
3) female college dropout, working in low-status manual job
4) male drug dealer, unemployed ⎫ all had poor employment
5) male drug dealer, unemployed ⎬ records, of manual jobs and
6) male drug dealer, unemployed ⎭ protracted voluntary unemployment

7) male graduate, temporarily unemployed
8) female student.

I do not suggest that those who were interviewed were representative of those who refused to co-operate. My observations suggest that the general lifestyles of all those who refused to be interviewed were similar to those of their friends who did co-operate. Five of the eight refusals provided me with a certain amount of biographical information during informal discussions which revealed that in their backgrounds and outlooks they appeared to resemble many of those included in the survey.

Many of the problems of the survey method are problems of sampling or choosing a representative group within a population. It was decided at an early stage in the present research not to attempt a random sample. This means that there are no grounds to justify generalization beyond the data collected. The method chosen was a self-selected non-random group of drugtakers whom I located through a network of friends. This technique is called 'snowballing'. This probably produced a biased selection, missing some important groups of drugtakers altogether, and missing isolates.

M. Plant (1975), *Drugtakers in an English Town*, pp. 13–14, 18–19, 20.

Questions

1. What sampling problems are raised by studies of drugtakers?
2. What is 'snowball sampling'? Examine the advantages and disadvantages of this approach to sampling.
3. Critically evaluate the sampling procedures used in Martin Plant's study.

☐ Theoretical Sampling

An alternative to statistical sampling is theoretical sampling – an approach devised by the American sociologists Barney Glaser and Anselm Strauss. This procedure is often discussed by methodologists, but rarely outlined in practice.

Reading 4

Quantitative research is concerned to establish that respondents are representative of a wider population, so that the generalizability of findings can be enhanced. In fact, much research departs significantly from this ideal in a number of ways. However, there is a case for suggesting that the issue of representativeness confronts the qualitative researcher too. The avowal to see through the eyes of one's subjects can be interpreted to imply that the ethnographer needs to attend to the question of the typicality of the eyes through which he or she is seeing. This kind of concern may be regarded as indicative of the application of an inappropriate criterion (that is, one deriving from the framework of quantitative research) to the ethnographer's mode of research. For example, in their exposition of grounded theory, Glaser and Strauss (1967) advocate that the qualitative research should give less attention to the need to meet statistical sampling criteria in assessing the adequacy of a 'sample'; rather, the researcher should be much more concerned with the issue of whether the sample conforms to the investigator's emerging theoretical framework. For example, in an ethnographic study of power in a medical school in the USA, Bucher (1970, p. 5) proposed that, following a preliminary analysis of her initial observations, 'data are being sought from areas of the organization which should provide test cases, so to speak, for emerging propositions'. According to the principles of 'theoretical sampling' (the term coined by Glaser and Strauss), the researcher observes only as many activities, or interviews as many people, as are needed in order to 'saturate' the categories being developed, and then turns to the next theoretical issue and carries out the same process over again. Thus the question of the adequacy of a sample is determined by the degree to which it permits the qualitative researcher to develop and confirm one or more categories; as soon as the researcher feels satisfied that the theoretical point has been established, he or she can move on to the next issue. This procedure allows the constant interplay between theory and research that Glaser and Strauss are keen to develop.

A. Bryman (1988), *Quantity and Quality in Social Research*, pp. 116–17.

Questions

1. In what ways do principles of sampling relate to quantitative and qualitative research?
2. What do you understand by 'theoretical sampling'?
3. What are the implications of theoretical sampling for the researcher's activities?

☐ Time Sampling

Within some studies researchers wish to sample the activities that occur over time. Accordingly, systematic schedules are devised in relation to the observations that the researcher wishes to make. In this reading Margaret Stacey illustrates the way in which observations were made of children in hospital.

Reading 5

Time sampling methods were developed by child psychologists in the 1930's for the observation of children. With the assistance of others the relevant child cases were watched during all their waking hours. The universe which was sampled was their nominal waking day (7 a.m. to 7 p.m.). This was divided into 20-minute intervals, during 5 minutes of each of which the child's interaction was recorded in detail, each period of 5 seconds during that time being recorded separately. Figure 1 [see p. 36] shows a record sheet. This method of recording concentrated on the time spent and told little about the quality of the interaction. More was learned about this by the diary method. The "hard" observations provided by the time sample were an excellent check on the more non-statistical and qualitative data.

M. Stacey (1969), *Methods of Social Research*, p. 64.

Questions

1. What do you understand by 'time sampling'?
2. Critically evaluate the observation sheet used by Margaret Stacey and her colleagues. How do the categories influence data collection?
3. Devise an observation sheet to engage in time sampling in a one hour sociology class. (Consider the time interval and the categories to be used.)

☐ Using Informants

A major feature of field studies has been the way in which researchers have worked in depth with a selection of the group they are studying. In these circumstances, consideration needs to be given to the criteria used to select informants. In this reading, I discuss the way in which I selected informants in my study of Bishop McGregor School.

Reading 6

Many researchers have indicated that their encounters with individuals who became key informants occurred by 'chance' and or

NAME ....

Date .... Day ....

People in Ward at beginning of sample ....

Time	Child on own	Position	Interaction with other children	Interaction with nurses		Interaction with other people (doctors, sister, domestic, technicians, porters, parents, - specify)		Who comes into Ward and who leaves
				As individual	As one of group	As individual	As one of group	
1								1
2								2
3								3
4								4
5								5
6								6

Designed by R. Pill

Figure 1 **Observation sheet**

that they were people who they got to know particularly well or with whom they became friends. While I would not deny that these are dimensions of my research encounters I would also argue that some account has to be taken of who becomes a key informant, their sex, status and role, if the researcher is to exercise some control over the collection of data. At Bishop McGregor School I kept a record of my informants and of my key informants in order that I could examine the pattern that emerged.

As Table 1 [see p. 38] indicates there were twelve teachers whom I regarded as regular informants, five of whom became key informants; that is teachers with whom I had a more intense relationship. All of these teachers provided a high level of co-operation with my research. However, I draw a distinction between informants and key informants on the basis of my contact with them, their commitment to my work and assistance with the project on a regular basis. It was the key informants whom I got to know best and who helped me to orientate my research questions, and my observations. In working with both informants and key informants I attempted to ensure that I had a cross-section of teaching staff in terms of age, sex, level of seniority, teaching experience, post of responsibility and areas of the school from which they were drawn. In these terms, I attempted to maintain some balance between the individuals with whom I worked. Furthermore, I tried to take into account the areas of the school to which they would give access. Of the informants with whom I worked there were individuals who represented academic subject departments, practical subjects and the Newsom Department. While I would argue that I obtained a cross-section of teachers on this basis, I think those teachers whom I got to know best tended to be concentrated more towards the arts subjects than the sciences. However, among these teachers I did have people with a range of teaching experiences which included probationary teachers, junior teachers, middle ranking teachers (who were deputy heads of departments) and a head of department. Meanwhile, beyond them in the teaching hierarchy my key informants included Heads of Houses and the headmaster.

On this basis I would argue that my informants, including key informants, constituted a cross-section of the teaching staff. Yet I cannot argue that they were purposely selected, for in some cases they included teachers who had attached themselves to me when I joined the school or when they joined the school. However, I monitored the kinds of people with whom I talked throughout the research period in order to take account of the different perspectives and different versions of the school to which I was exposed by my key informants.

R.G. Burgess (1985), 'In the Company of Teachers: key informants in the study of a

Table 1 Key informants and informants at Bishop McGregor School

Name	Sex	Status/teaching experience	Post in school	House/department
Key informants				
Sylvia Robinson	Female	Teacher of ten years experience with head of department status	Head of Careers in charge of Newsom Scale III	Careers/Newsom
Maggie Rolls	Female	Head of House (a senior teacher but junior in terms of age)	Head of House Scale V	House
Paul Klee	Male	Probationer (new to the school)	Scale I	English
Ron Ward	Male	New Head of House	Head of House Scale V	House
Geoff Goddard	Male		Headmaster	A variety of teaching duties
Informants				
Jane Adams	Female	Departy head of department	Scale III	English
George Jackson	Male	Head of department	Scale V	English
Keith Dryden	Male	Junior assistant teacher in departments	Scale II	Art/Newsom
Tony Davis	Male	Junior assistant teacher in departments	Scale II	Craft/Newsom
Terry Goodwin	Female	Junior assistant teacher in departments	Scale II	Home Economics/Newsom
Gerry Cochrane	Male	Probationer (new to the school)	Scale I	Religious Education
Michael O'Donoghue	Male	Assistant teacher in charge of a subject	Scale III	Science

Note: Teacher posts were graded one to five at the time of the study.

comprehensive school' in R.G. Burgess (ed), *Strategies of Educational Research*, pp. 89–91.

Questions

1. What are 'key informants'? Assess the value of their use by researchers.
2. Using the table in this reading, list the criteria involved in the selection of key informants and informants in the study.
3. What kinds of data would we need to check my statement that the key informants were a cross-section of the teaching staff?

□ Sampling Events

Researchers often focus on particular events and situations within their studies. This is particularly the case in field research where investigators focus on events such as christenings, weddings, and funerals, as well as dramatic events. In this reading, Schatzman and Strauss discuss the kind of events that the researcher can sample.

Reading 7

Another dimension that the researcher finds very important concerns *events or situations*. In truth, this dimension is at the heart of his research in so far as time, place, and even people represent – sociologically speaking – merely a context for situations and activities. There is a universe of situations or events from which the researcher can sample. Generally speaking, events or situations are of three orders: routine, special, and untoward. To the extent the human organization that he is studying is institutionalized, it will undoubtedly have many routine events, but even social movements will have some of these. Routine events are regularly scheduled situations wherein people meet to work or to discuss their activities. These situations include all regular meetings, conferences, and ordinary daily activities or work. Special events include fortuitous but anticipated occurrences, which, though not necessarily routine, are organized for moving the organization through successive stages of its activities. There are special meetings, outings, prearranged visits by outsiders, and the like. Untoward events include those that are entirely unanticipated, of an emergency nature, or to some extent anticipated but untimed. Clearly the situational dimension is highly interrelated with the temporal and spatial dimensions.

The easiest and most obvious procedure is to obtain lists of scheduled events that occur during any given period, such as a week, and selectively sample each event. Situations are, in fact, of such critical importance that the researcher might not even sample; he might take the entire universe – so that he is assured of having observed at least once every routine event which occurs in the organization. Later, he can establish the importance of any of these events, and decide how many successive visits and observations he would need before he could fully understand the implications of each event. In the course of these visits and participations, the researcher will hear of special events upcoming and will take pains to attend and observe at these, for he can expect that special events have special implications for the participants. To the extent that either is at any given location within the organization or moving about, he is in a position to witness untoward events. And if not actually there in the midst of a unique occurrence, he will have people at hand with whom he can speak about what had actually occurred – usually picking up a variety of perspectives on any given occurrence. He can maximize this variety by seeking out persons whom he anticipates might have differential perspectives, including those that represent people low in hierarchy or tending to hold marginal or "peculiar" views.

L. Schatzman and A. Strauss (1973), *Field Research: Strategies for a Natural Sociology*, pp. 42–3.

Questions

1. What do you understand by 'routine events', 'special events' and 'untoward events'? Give examples of each event.
2. How can routine events be sampled?
3. Consider ways in which you could study routine events, special events and untoward events in the community in which you live.

Project Questions

1. Design a sample survey of a housing estate or village in your locality. What issues and problems of sampling do you have to consider?
2. Consider the kinds of studies you could conduct where snowball sampling might be appropriate.
3. What key informants could be used in a sociological study of your school or college? Consider the criteria that would be used when studying:
   (a) the lunch break
   (b) games lessons
   (c) the sixth form or student common room.

Further Reading

Many of the volumes listed below are very detailed. In particular, students are recommended to read Sara Arber's chapter in Gilbert (1993), while those doing survey work are recommended to read the practical approach to sampling discussed by de Vaus (1986).

A. Boehm and R.A. Weinberg, *The Classroom Observer: A Guide for Developing Observational Skills* (Teachers College Press, 1977), provides a discussion of time and event sampling.

R.G. Burgess, *In The Field: An Introduction to Field Research* (Allen and Unwin, 1984), contains a chapter on selection in field research.

J. Casagrande (ed), *In the Company of Man* (Harper and Row, 1960), is a classic set of accounts on key informants.

P. Croll, *Systematic Classroom Observation* (Falmer Press, 1986), provides a good guide to classroom observation schedules based on time samples.

D.A. de Vaus, *Surveys in Social Research* (Allen and Unwin, 1986), contains a good practical guide to sampling in survey research.

N. Gilbert (ed), *Researching Social Life* (Sage, 1993), includes a chapter by Sara Arber on designing samples that provides a very good summary of issues concerned with different types of sampling.

B.G. Glaser and A.L. Strauss, *The Discovery of Grounded Theory* (Aldine, 1967), is the original work on which discussions of grounded theory are based.

4 | Experiments in social research

In the popular imagination the word 'experiment' is equated with the world of natural science, especially laboratory work in physics and chemistry. However, numerous books and studies suggest that an attempt can be made to apply the logic of the methods of investigation used in natural science to research in the social sciences. Such an investigation would involve separating a population into an experimental group and a control group with a view to identifying the effects of the exposure of the experimental group to the experimental condition. While most sociologists do not use experiments in their research, it does not mean that the *logic* of the experiment is not used. As Bulmer (1984) has shown, 'Non experimental research designs attempt to identify causal relationships' (p. 9). He suggests that several variations have occurred in research designs that relate to the experimental ideal. They are:

a the single case study of one group over a period of time;
b the static group comparison where data are collated from two or more groups which differ in their exposure to a variable;
c studying a sample at one point in time followed by another sample at another point in time;
d the longitudinal study that follows a selected group of individuals over time.

The language and associated issues within experimental studies are therefore present in other research designs where comparison and causality are involved. The 'classic experiment' involves comparisons between what happens in a control group and what happens in an experimental group. In particular, experiments are concerned with internal validity, that is whether the experimental variable has had the effect observed, and external validity, that is whether the findings can be generalised.

But can social scientists conduct true experiments? Some psychologists and social psychologists have conducted experiments in laboratory situations. For example, experiments have been conducted on the effects of authority on human behaviour. Meanwhile, in the field of education, where researchers wish to examine the effect of a particular teaching method, experimental studies may be conducted. However, this approach is not without problems when people become part of an experimental situation. In these circumstances the key question is whether people behave in experimental situations as they do in natural settings.

The experimental effect is often called the 'Hawthorne effect' after a classic study that took place in the Hawthorne plant of the General Electric Company. Here, it was found that the experiment itself had a crucial effect on the outcome of the project. This theme can be explored in greater detail when considering the kinds of cues that experimenters 'give off ' to their subjects. Such situations provide a series of lessons for those researchers who work within an ethnographic tradition where consideration has to be given to the effect of the researcher on the researched in a field setting.

Some researchers have conducted experiments in natural settings. These field experiments often take place in a social context without the knowledge of those involved. In this respect, such field experiments are examples of covert research. A classic field experiment was conducted by Rosenhan and his colleagues (Rosenhan, 1973) who wanted to know whether the symptoms associated with mental illness were recognised by medical practitioners. Accordingly, the researchers presented themselves to mental hospitals as patients who then behaved 'normally' in order to see how long it would take to be discharged as cured. While they were eventually discharged, none of these pseudopatients were discharged as 'cured'.

There are other types of experimental approach. First, the 'quasi experiment' which is an approximation of an experiment where non-randomly selected groups act as the control. Ideally, such groups are similar on all the variables that may affect the outcome that is being assessed. Secondly, there are 'ethnomethodological experiments'. Such experiments examine what happens when particular activities take place. This 'experiment' is not based upon the hypothetico-deductive method, but needs to be considered among the repertoire of experimental approaches that can be used by social scientists.

All the readings in this chapter are provided to encourage readers to consider the implications of the experiment and experimental effects on other aspects of the research process: research design, relationships between researcher and researched and the ethics of social research.

☐ The Classic Experiment

The characteristics of the classic experiment are summarised by Sanders and Pinhey who provide a guide to the key concepts associated with this approach.

Reading 1

The following diagram and summary constitute all of the features and steps in the classic experiment.

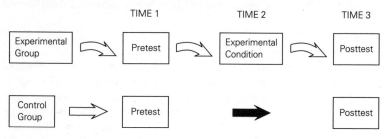

| | TIME 1 | TIME 2 | TIME 3 |

Step 1   Select a control and experimental group using matching and/or random assignment.
Step 2   Give the control and experimental groups a pretest.
Step 3   Introduce the experimental variable to the experimental group and do nothing to the control group.
Step 4   Administer the posttest (same instrument used in the pretest) to both the control and experimental groups.
Step 5   Compare the results of the posttests to determine the effect, if any, of the experimental variable. The differences are assumed to be caused by the experimental variable since that was the only difference between the two groups between the pretest and posttest.

W.B. Sanders and T.K. Pinhey (1983), *The Conduct of Social Research*, pp. 168–9.

Questions

1. Using the terms in the diagram, design a classic experiment in an area of social life of your choice.
2. What are the advantages and disadvantages of experimental studies?
3. What do you understand by
   (a) internal validity
   (b) external validity? (see the introduction to this chapter.)

☐ Conducting Classical Experiments

Classical experimental designs involve a particular sequence. Sanders discusses the sequence involved and assesses its utility in particular situations.

Reading 2

The sequence of operation for the classical experiment begins with a hypothesis. For example, an educator might hypothesize that, if students are given positive encouragement, they will perform better in a learning task – say, mastering a list of spelling words. In order to test this hypothesis experimentally, the researcher would take a group of students who were equal in academic ability and divide them into a control group and an experimental group. Next, the researcher would test each group to make sure they were equal. This is the pretest. In this case, the researcher might use a spelling test as a pretest. Next, the researcher introduces the experimental variable, positive encouragement – for instance, saying a kind word – but only to the experimental group. He would not give the control group positive encouragement of any sort. Both groups would be treated the same in every other way, with the sole exception that *only* members of the experimental group would receive encouragement. Finally, the two groups would be tested a second time on the list of spelling words to find whether there were any performance differences between them. If there is a difference, and all other aspects of the composition of the group and the experimental procedure were held constant, the difference can be attributed to the experimental variable – that is, the experimental variable can be said to have caused the difference.

The classical experimental design has been highly successful in the natural sciences, and it has therefore been widely used in social research as well. Unlike natural scientists, however, sociologists deal with a subject matter that has a mind of its own, and they have therefore encountered problems not found in the natural sciences.

W.B. Sanders (1976), *The Sociologist as Detective*, pp. 141–2.

Questions

1. What do you understand by the terms
   (a) dependent variable
   (b) independent variable?

2. Give an example of an independent variable causing a change in the dependent variable in an area of social life.
3. What would be the ethical and political problems associated with conducting the spelling experiment in a class in your school or college?

☐ The Hawthorne Effect

Researchers who are engaged in experimental studies need to be sure that the effects are not those of the experiment being conducted. This is known as the Hawthorne effect (named after the company where it was originally identified).

Reading 3

There are other sets of factors more difficult to account for, which are, the effects of the experiment itself: a series of effects known as 'control effects'. Researchers became alerted to these during a long-term research programme carried out between 1927 and 1932 at the Western Electric Company's Hawthorne plant in Chicago. One aim of the study was to examine the effects of various changes in working conditions on the output of a group of girl workers so that it could be determined which set of conditions were the most satisfactory in creating high output. Six girls were chosen for the experiment. They were chosen as average workers, neither inexperienced nor terribly expert. Their work consisted of the assembly of telephone relays. The girls were taken to a test room divided from the main work area. Care was taken to make sure that the output rate, as something easily measured in terms of units produced, was unaffected by factors extraneous to the experiment. The number of faulty parts, the weather each day, the state of health of the girls and so on were all recorded so that they could be taken into account during analysis. The nature of the experiment was carefully explained to the girls, and every effort was made to allay any of their natural anxieties. Whenever an experimental change was planned, the girls were fully informed and their comments requested – and received. Throughout the study, they were repeatedly told not to strain themselves unduly, but to continue working at a pace they felt comfortable. For a two-week period prior to entering the test room, the output of each girl was measured, without her knowledge, while she was working in the regular production setting. For five weeks after the girls had entered the test room, no change was made in the working conditions. In this way, the investigators hoped to notice any changes in output attributable to transfer from the regular assembly room to the test room. A third period involved a change in the method of payment. Some eight weeks later, two rest periods of five minutes each were introduced. Six five-minute periods were established in the next experimental period. Other changes introduced at various stages were light lunches at company expense, earlier clocking-off, and a five-day working week, each change lasting some weeks.

The results, in terms of the output curve, were somewhat surprising. Throughout the period of the experiment, the output curve had risen slowly but steadily. Even when weekly output fell on the introduction of a five-day week, daily output still increased. The researchers, trying to find a control, for a twelve-week period returned conditions to what they had been originally. Output rose higher than ever!

The conclusion forced on the researchers was that, in this case at least, output did not seem to depend upon working conditions, otherwise returning to the original conditions of work should have caused output to decline to its original level. Certain other conditions were also repeated, and in no case did the output from identical conditions remain the same. Indeed, the only apparent uniformity was the increase in output through each successive experimental period. The experimenters concluded that the increase in the output curve was reflecting something other than the responses of the group to the experimental stimuli. But what? Many possible factors were ruled out. There were no errors caused by inadequate matching, since the group functioned, as was thought, as its own control. History was ruled out, since the girls were working in a contrived setting under isolated and carefully controlled conditions and because various supplementary records indicated otherwise.

After ruling out other possible explanations, with a certain inevitability the researchers concluded that the experiment itself was confounding the intended aim of their study. Questioning the girls afterwards, the researchers discovered that each girl knew she was producing more than when she was working in the regular assembly shop. It seemed easier, it seemed fun, and they were able to work in a relaxed atmosphere away from the normal supervisory control. In addition, the girls knew they were taking part in an important and interesting experiment, the results of which could, in some way, lead to an improvement in working conditions in the plant as a whole. The researchers had, from the beginning, taken pains to acquaint the girls with what was going on, to reassure them and, very different from their normal work routine, to consult them. In short, the very act of research had generated processes in the group so that output was recording not the physical conditions of the work setting, but the social development of the group itself. Over the period of the experiment, the group of girls developed a cohesion and a pattern of relationships, including leadership roles, friendship bonds (which often continued after hours) and reciprocal ties, none of which had been particularly apparent before the girls became subjects in the experiment. In a way, the members of the group developed common purposes, and soon after the inception of the study had committed themselves to a continuous increase in output.

The importance of these developments for experiments in general is that they are not the traditional kind of coincidental changes which could have occurred apart from the conditions imposed by the research, *but were a result of the research itself.* By isolating the girls, and by heightening their awareness that they were under study, thereby enhancing their sense of importance, the researchers changed the very action they wanted to study. Interestingly, this discovery of the relationship between the development of an informal group structure and group productivity was to become one of the major findings of the research and was the start of a massive reorientation in the study of work group dynamics. But, in addition, the interest for methodology is that it alerted researchers to one important factor which could influence the results of research: the research itself.

J. Hughes (1976), *Sociological Analysis*, pp. 94–7.

Questions

1. Draw a diagram to summarise the key phases of the Hawthorne experiment.
2. Write a short paragraph to summarise the key characteristics of the Hawthorne Effect.
3. What do you consider are the implications of this study for other forms of social research?

☐ A Field Experiment

This reading provides a classic account of a field experiment where eight sane people gained admission to psychiatric hospitals in order to discover how diagnosis occurred among patients.

Reading 4

The eight pseudopatients were a varied group. One was a psychology graduate student in his 20s. The remaining seven were older and 'established'. Among them were three psychologists, a pediatrician, a psychiatrist, a painter, and a housewife. Three pseudopatients were women, five were men. All of them employed pseudonyms, lest their alleged diagnoses embarrass them later. Those who were in mental health professions alleged another occupation in order to avoid the special attentions that might be accorded by staff, as a matter of courtesy or caution, to ailing colleagues. With the exception of myself (I was the first pseudopatient and my presence was known to the hospital administrator and chief psychologist and, so far as I can tell, to them alone), the presence of pseudopatients and the nature of the research program was not known to the hospital staff.

The settings were similarly varied. In order to generalise the findings, admission into a variety of hospitals was sought. The 12 hospitals in the sample were located in five different states on the East and West coasts. Some were old and shabby, some were quite new. Some were research-oriented, others not. Some had good staff–patient ratios, others were quite understaffed. Only one was a strictly private hospital. All of the others were supported by state or federal state funds or, in one instance, by university funds.

After calling the hospital for an appointment, the pseudopatient arrived at the admissions office complaining that he had been hearing voices. Asked what the voices said, he replied that they were often unclear, but as far as he could tell they said 'empty', 'hollow', and 'thud'. The voices were unfamiliar and were of the same sex as the pseudopatient. The choice of these symptoms was occasioned by their apparent similarity to existential symptoms. Such symptoms are alleged to arise from painful concerns about the perceived meaninglessness of one's life. It is as if the hallucinating person were saying, 'My life is empty and hollow'. The choice of these symptoms was also determined by the *absence* of a single report of existential psychoses in the literature.

Beyond alleging the symptoms and falsifying name, vocation, and employment, no further alterations of person, history, or circumstances were made. The significant events of the pseudopatient's life were presented as they had actually occurred. Relationships with parents and siblings, with spouse and children, with people at work and in school, consistent with the aforementioned exceptions, were described as they were or had been. Frustrations and upsets were described along with joys and satisfactions. These facts are important to remember. If anything, they strongly biased the subsequent results in favor of detecting sanity, since none of their histories or current behaviors were seriously pathological in any way.

Immediately upon admission to the psychiatric ward, the pseudopatient ceased simulating *any* symptoms of abnormality. In some cases, there was a brief period of mild nervousness and anxiety, since none of the pseudopatients really believed that they would be admitted so easily. Indeed, their shared fear was that they would be immediately exposed as frauds and greatly embarrassed. Moreover, many of them had never visited a psychiatric ward; even those who had, nevertheless had some genuine fears about what might happen to them. Their nervousness, then, was quite appropriate to the novelty of the hospital setting, and it abated rapidly.

Apart from the short-lived nervousness, the pseudopatient behaved on the ward as he 'normally' behaved. The pseudopatient spoke to patients and staff as he might ordinarily. Because there is uncommonly little to do on a psychiatric ward, he attempted to engage others in conversation. When asked by staff how he was feeling, he indicated that he was fine, that he no longer experienced symptoms. He responded to instructions from attendants, to calls for medication (which was not swallowed), and to dining-hall instructions. Beyond such activities as were available to him on the admissions ward, he spent his time writing down his observations about the ward, its patients, and the staff. Initially these notes were written 'secretly', but as it soon became clear that no one much cared, they were subsequently written on standard tablets of paper in such public places as the dayroom. No secret was made of these activities.

The pseudopatient, very much as a true psychiatric patient, entered a hospital with no foreknowledge of when he would be discharged. Each was told that he would have to get out by his own devices, essentially by convincing the staff that he was sane. The psychological stresses associated with hospitalisation were considerable, and all but one of the pseudopatients desired to be discharged almost immediately after being admitted. They were, therefore, motivated not only to behave sanely, but to be paragons of co-operation. That their behavior was in no way disruptive is confirmed by nursing reports, which have been obtained on most of the patients. These reports uniformly indicate that the patients were 'friendly', 'co-operative', and 'exhibited no abnormal indications'.

M. Rosenhan (1982), 'On Being Sane in Insane Places' in M. Bulmer (ed), *Social Research Ethics*, pp.17–19.

Questions

1. List the characteristics of this study that constitute an experiment.
2. What are the ethical problems associated with this study?
3. Design a field experiment that you could conduct in your school or college.

□ A Quasi-experiment

As true experiments are difficult to conduct in sociology, many investigators have attempted to engage in quasi-experiments by comparing the before and after situation or a situation in a group where a change has occurred with one where no such change has happened.

Reading 5

In 1973, the New Zealand Council for Educational Research began work on a research project concerned with the effects of a 'book flood' on the reading habits, tastes and abilities of school children. Two schools with an intake aged from 5 years to 11 years were involved in the study. Over half of their intake were Maori children many of whom were said to have 'limited access to books'. Suitable books were selected by a committee of teachers and librarians and introduced into the schools over a period of two terms. To assess the impact of the flood of books, a series of baseline assessments of reading skills and attitudes were obtained between March and May 1976 before the books arrived and then again six months after the initial influx of books had taken place. The pretest battery included tests of reading comprehension, vocabulary and listening, and scales to assess children's interests in books, attitudes to school, to reading and to themselves. The amount of reading undertaken in a two-week period was recorded by the children themselves and teachers' ratings of interest in reading were also obtained. Case studies were made of five children in each class and information was obtained about the books the children owned and had read, their home background, parental interest, library borrowing and TV viewing. Finally, informal reading inventories were used to study the children's reading behaviour.

The effects of the book flood were analysed in terms of the amount of reading undertaken by the children during the course of the project, their reading skills, reading interests and their attitudes toward reading in general.

Using the symbols and conventions adopted earlier (p. 188) to represent research designs, we can illustrate the New Zealand study as:

(Experimental) $O_1 \quad X \quad O_2$

The briefest consideration reveals inadequacies in the design. Indeed, Campbell and Stanley described *the one group pretest-post-test design* as 'a "bad example" to illustrate several of the confounded extraneous variables that can jeopardize internal validity. These variables offer plausible hypotheses explaining an O_1–O_2 difference, rival to the hypothesis that caused the difference'.

Nevertheless, the New Zealand researchers confidently report that the first six months of the book flood produced significant changes in the amount of their subjects' voluntary reading, and improvements in their reading abilities, attitudes and interests.

A Quasi-experimental Design

The Bradford Book Flood Experiment began in 1976 with two aims in view. First, to study the effects of a book flood on children's reading abilities and interests. Second, to improve upon the research design used in the New Zealand study within the limits imposed by funding and the requests that could be made for changes in the timetabling and day-to-day organisation of the participating schools. The design finally adopted by the Bradford research team after considerable discussion may be represented thus:

(Experimental) $O_1 \quad X \quad O_2$
(Control) $O_3 \qquad O_4$

It is, of course, the *non-equivalent control group design* in which the parallel rows separated by the dashed line represent groups that have not been equated by random assignment.

Four middle schools took part in the Bradford study, two serving as experimental and two as control schools. Two schools forming a matched pair were situated on council estates, the second matched pair being located in inner city areas. Allocation to experiment or control treatments was made on the flip of a coin.

The schools were selected by a senior educational adviser who attempted to choose schools of similar size, background, organisation, teaching methods and catering for children of a similar range of abilities. Unlike the New Zealand study, the Bradford research followed one particular year group (second year pupils) through the school. Pretest and post-test measures of reading skills, attitudes and interests were supplemented by classroom observation and interviews with selected children, the analysis of diaries and reading record forms, and the use of teachers' assessments. In the light of the problems of *instrumentation* to which we referred earlier, particular care was taken to select reading tests that: (1) had been recently constructed or recently restandardised; (2) had British norms; (3) were reliable and valid; (4) were suitable for the age group under study; and (5) were appropriate over the two-year testing sessions. Unlike the New Zealand study, the Bradford design attempted to use both matching and random allocation (of a sort) to obtain equivalent groups at the outset of the research. Despite this, the study remains firmly quasi-experimental rather than experimental since random allocation to experimental and control groups at the level of individual pupils was clearly impossible and what random allocation did take place at the level of institutions was of little consequence because of the small number of schools involved. Although the Bradford investigators attempted to exercise control over extraneous variables, it is not difficult to criticise the study in respect of each of the threats to internal and external validity that we identified earlier. For example, the matching of schools that was undertaken was relatively crude and did not take account of the important variations in the intrasessional histories of the schools that participated. Of equal import, it does not appear that a precise, unequivocal description of the experimental treatment was ever undertaken. What exactly constitutes a book flood? One could go on raising aspects of design weakness which jeopardise the validity of the Bradford research project, but such criticisms would serve only to reinforce the point that true experimentation in education is rarely, if ever, achieved.

L. Cohen and L. Manion (1989), *Research Methods in Education*, pp. 200–2.

Questions

1. Why is the Bradford study a 'quasi-experiment'?
2. Do you think the Bradford design improved on the New Zealand study? Give reasons for your answer.
3. How could you design a similar study in your town or city?

☐ An Ethnomethodological Experiment

Ethnomethodological experiments involve 'happenings' that are designed to elicit reactions from those involved so that the investigator can record the reactions.

Reading 6

Any time we do something that others regard as strange behavior in our usual routine of everyday affairs, we are probably violating some norm. The person who laughs and talks to herself or himself is violating a well-understood and widely recognized norm, and the stares, scowls, and finger pointing of other persons serve as punishment or negative sanctions to bring his or her behavior back in line. Once when I was a graduate student I experienced an incident that I am still unsure how to label. I was having lunch at a table in the cafeteria of the student union. I was alone, and had a partially filled glass of water on the table. A young man suddenly appeared through the door from the kitchen area of the cafeteria, grabbed my glass of water, and retreated into the kitchen with it. Since I was aware of ethnomethodological experiments of this sort that had the character of "happenings" but were designed to elicit a reaction on the part of the victim and record how he reacted, I thought at the time that this was a project for an undergraduate sociology class. I never found out for certain, though, and I also thought it could be the work of a practical joker or of a "crazy" person, as some of the cafeteria workers were from the state mental hospital. It was certainly a puzzling occurrence, and the only way to ascertain what it meant, or to explain it so as to relieve the ambiguity and puzzlement in my mind, was to label it in some form, such as the work of a joker, crazy person, or social researcher.

Garfinkel (1967) reports a variety of experiments he has designed to demonstrate to students the existence of such norms, and to observe and record the behaviors of others when the student violates the norms. In one such experiment Garfinkel required undergraduate students to spend from 15 minutes to an hour viewing the interaction within their homes as if they were boarders or strangers in the household, rather than playing their usual role as familiar family members. Students were instructed only to observe, not actually to act as strangers. Their written reports of what they observed did not take into account any usual "insider's" commonsense knowledge of household history, and references to subjective elements such as imputed motive were omitted. From their vantage point as "boarders," the students were surprised to see the way family members treated one another. The whole atmosphere was one of private rather than public behavior, with little respect for table manners, apparent freedom to criticize others, and a general absence of impression management. The students generally felt that the boarder's account did not represent their "real" home environment (Garfinkel 1967, p. 46).

In the next experiment students spent from 15 minutes to an hour not only assuming they were boarders but actually acting out this assumption. In approximately 80 percent of the cases family members reacted strongly to restore the situation to normal. Family members (who did not know what was happening) were bewildered, anxious, and embarrassed. Students were told by family members that they were being inconsiderate, selfish, and impolite. Students were asked if they were sick, stupid, or mad, or questions such as "What has gotten into you?"

K.D. Bailey (1978), *Methods of Social Research*, pp. 256–7.

Questions

1. Explain what you understand to be the key characteristics of an ethnomethodological experiment.
2. Compare and contrast ethnomethodological experiments and classic experiments.
3. Evaluate the evidence available from Garfinkel's ethnomethodological experiments.

Project Questions

1. Outline the research design for an experiment in your school or college.
2. Consider the ethical problems involved in the experiment you have designed.
3. Design an ethnomethodological experiment that you can conduct in your school or college and assess the difficulties involved in conducting it.

Further Reading

P. Aggleton, *Health* (Routledge, 1990), contains a discussion of HIV research that relies on the comparative method.

A. Bryman, *Quantity and Quality in Social Research* (Unwin Hyman, 1988), provides numerous entries on the experiment as a quantitative method. See the index.

M. Bulmer (ed), *Sociological Research Methods* (Macmillan, 1988; 2nd Edition). The introduction contains a useful discussion of experiments in relation to research design.

D.T. Campbell and J.C. Stanley, *Experimental and Quasi-Experimental Designs* (Rand McNally, 1986), is the classic study.

H. Garfinkel, *Studies in Ethnomethodology* (Prentice Hall, 1967), provides the definitive account of ethnomethodology through a collection of essays.

C. Haney, C. Banks and P. Zimbardo, 'A Study of Prisoners and Guards in a Simulated Prison' in D. Potter *et al.*, *Society and the Social Sciences: An Introduction* (Routledge and Kegan Paul, 1981), provides an account of social science experiments.

P. McNeill, *Research Methods* (Routledge, 1990; 2nd Edition), provides a very clear account of experiments – very readable for students.

S. Milgram, 'Some Conditions of Obedience and Disobedience to Authority' in *Human Relations*, Vol. 18 (1965), pp. 57–74, is a classic study of a social science experiment on authority and obedience.

D. Reynolds and M. Sullivan with S. Murgatroyd, *The Comprehensive Experiment* (Falmer Press, 1987). Chapter 3 on research design reviews the problems of experiments in social research

5 | Conducting surveys

Survey research is probably the research method which is best known by members of the general public. Surveys are often included in newspapers and magazines where readers are persuaded to return their responses in exchange for a gift. In addition, individuals are often stopped in the street by interviewers working for market-research companies.

Many social researchers engage in social surveys. These may be conducted in a variety of ways: through face to face interviews, through postal surveys and through telephone interviews. In each case the researcher has to consider carefully a number of issues which include:

a formulating a field of study
b choosing a questionnaire
c piloting a survey
d finalising the questionnaire
e conducting the survey.

While it is possible to write about the principles associated with each phase of a survey, it is easier to discuss these issues in relation to an actual study. Here, emphasis will be given to the design of the questionnaire as this will be a practical concern for many readers conducting small-scale studies.

A study in which I have been involved was a comparative survey of secondary school teachers in England and Japan, and so all examples will be taken from this survey. The project was designed to look at educational reforms and the teaching profession. The intention was to conduct a survey of all secondary school teachers in Coventry in the United Kingdom and Amagasaki City in Japan. These cities were chosen as they are both similar in size and have a similar compositon in terms of social class groups.

As all secondary school teachers were to be contacted in this study, a postal questionnaire was designed. Each questionnaire contained a statement to introduce the survey in the following terms:

This questionnaire is part of the collaborative international research project between CEDAR, University of Warwick and Osaka Kyoiku University in Japan. The research is being conducted in Coventry and Amagasaki City, Japan, to investigate impacts of current educational reforms upon secondary schools both in the UK and Japan. The information which you provide will form a very important part of the project and will help us to contribute to an understanding of secondary education in both countries.

This questionnaire is to be completed anonymously. It will be analysed statistically, and all the information will be treated in the strictest confidence. The findings of this survey will be made known through a survey report which will be sent to all schools involved in this research project.

Please answer questions by circling the appropriate number unless otherwise stated. Some open-ended questions invite you to write short answers to explore more complex issues. When you have completed this questionnaire, please fold it and place it in the collection box provided in your school.

It should be noted that the statement included details of the organisations conducting the study, the purpose of the survey, the way in which the data would be treated confidentially and instructions for the completion and collection of the questionnaire.

Within the questionnaire different kinds of questions were designed. First, closed questions that provided individuals with the answers from which they could choose their response. These included questions requesting biographical information:

1   Please circle the appropriate number.
     a) Sex: b) Age: c) Status:

Male	1
Female	2

20 – 29	1
30 – 39	2
40 – 49	3
over 50	4

Full-time	1
Part-time	2

Such questions force the respondent to make a specific response, but may be complemented by an open-ended question which gives respondents an opportunity to explain what they are doing, as shown in the following example:

8a   Are you a form tutor this year?

(Please circle one number.)

Yes	1
No	2

8b   Do you have any other responsibilities in addition to teaching and/or being a tutor?

(Please circle one number.)

Yes	1
No	2

8c   If Yes, give a brief description.

....
....
....

As can be seen, such closed questions are pre-coded and are therefore as quick for the researcher to analyse as they are for the respondent to complete.

A different form of question used within the questionnaire involved a ranking scale. Here the respondent was invited to rank responses from a limited range of choices, as shown in the following example:

1   What changes have occurred in your workload in the last two academic years?

(Please circle one number on each line.)

	Increased considerably	Increased	No change	Decreased
a) Teaching load	1	2	3	4
b) Preparation for lessons	1	2	3	4
c) Marking and recording	1	2	3	4
d) Meetings	1	2	3	4
e) Other administrative work	1	2	3	4
f) INSET	1	2	3	4

A further type of question used in this questionnaire was open ended questions:

3b   In England 30 to 40% of the population stays on beyond the compulsory age whereas in Japan it is over 90%. What do you think the lower figure in England is due to?

. . . .

. . . .

. . . .

While such a question gives respondents maximum freedom to provide an answer, these responses can be difficult to code. On this basis, decisions have to be reached about whether codes should be attached to sets of responses or the data used in a qualitative way. No matter which approach is used, it is very time consuming and a costly element of the study.

Once the questionnaire for a study has been drafted, it needs to be piloted to discover if any changes are necessary. In the case of this study, the questionnaire was piloted with some secondary schoolteachers in Warwickshire who were invited to comment on the questions as well as completing their responses. On the basis of their responses the questionnaire was finalised before being circulated to the teachers to be studied.

Once completed, the survey was coded, analysed and used to produce reports and articles. These aspects of survey investigation are discussed in some detail in the readings which follow. Together these readings illustrate major aspects of survey investigation.

☐ What is a Survey?

Surveys are now commonly used by a variety of organisations, but we need to consider what constitutes a social survey. In this reading, Cathie Marsh outlines the key components of the social survey.

Reading 1

But before proceeding further, I must give some definition of what I mean by this word 'survey'. The word has a long tradition in the English language, and developed from being the fact of viewing or inspecting something in detail (as in a land survey) to the act of doing so rigorously and comprehensively, and finally to the written results. The idea of the social survey started with this connotation of the collection of social facts, but has undergone an evolution such that nowadays the survey method is not just a way of collecting data but also of analysing the results.

For the purposes of this book, *[The Survey Method]*, a survey refers to an investigation where:

(a) systematic measurements are made over a series of cases yielding a rectangle of data;
(b) the variables in the matrix are analysed to see if they show any patterns;
(c) the subject matter is social.

In other words, the surveys we shall be looking at have a particular method of data collection, a particular method of data analysis and a particular substance.

The only restriction made on the survey as a method of collecting data is to insist that it be systematic, looking at more than one *case*, be it individuals, hospitals, countries, or whatever, and measuring the same variables on each case, so that you end up with each case having one and only one code for each variable. The data could come from observation, from fixed-choice responses to a postal questionnaire, from content analysis of newspapers, or from postcoding tape-recorded depth interviews. The important thing is that there is more than one case and that variation between cases is considered systematically. 'Survey analysis' involves making casual inferences from some kind of passive observation programme. The word 'survey' *is* sometimes used to refer to such investigations as a split-ballot question-wording trial, where there has been an experimental manipulation, but I think it is clearer if we use the word 'experiment' to describe such investigations.

Surveys and experiments are the only two methods known to me to test a hypothesis about how the world works. The experimenter intervenes in the social world, does something to a set of subjects (and usually also refrains from doing that thing to a set of controls) and looks to see what effect *manipulating* variance in the independent variable has on the dependent variable. If the subjects have been assigned in some fashion to control and experimental groups, the experimenter can be sure that it is what she did to the independent variable that has produced any differences between the groups.

The survey researcher has only made a series of observations; to be sure, as we shall come on to argue, these cannot be seen as passive reflections of unproblematic reality, but they must be logically distinguished from the manipulation that the experimenter engages in. The only element of randomness in the survey design comes in random selection of cases; *random sampling does not achieve the same result as random allocation into control and experimental groups.* The survey researcher may have a theory which leads her to suspect that X is having a causal effect on Y. If she wants to test this, she has to measure X and Y on a variety of different subjects, and infer from the fact that X and Y covary that the original hypothesis was true. But unlike the experimenter, she cannot rule out the possibility *in principle* of there being a third variable prior to X and Y and causing the variance in both; the experimenter knows that the relationship is not spurious because she knows exactly what produced the variance in X – *she* did.

In other words, in survey research the process of testing causal hypotheses, central to any theory-building endeavour, is a very indirect process of drawing inferences from already existing variance in populations by a rigorous process of comparison. In practice, one of the major strategies of the survey researcher is to control for other variables that she thinks might realistically be held also to produce an effect, but she never gets round the purist's objection that she has not definitely established a causal relationship. Furthermore, although having panel data across time certainly helps with the practical resolution of the problem of how to decide which of one's variables are prior to which others, it does not solve the logical difficulty that, in principle, any relationship which one finds may be explained by the operation of another unmeasured factor.

Finally, the subject matter of the surveys that sociologists are interested in is always social. Many different disciplines collect systematic observational data and make inferences from it. Biologists looking at correlations between plant growth and different types of environment, psychologists coding films of mother–child interactions, or astronomers drawing inferences about the origins of the universe from measurements of light intensity taken now, are all performing activities whose logic is similar to that of the social survey analyst, but they would not describe their studies as 'surveys'. I once analysed the product of one week's cuttings from all references in the national and local newspapers and magazines to the world survey. This produced a list of very different activities described as 'surveys' – a building society investigating house values, a local authority checking up that hospitals were instituting adequate safety precautions, commercial surveys of different markets and so on.

C. Marsh (1982), *The Survey Method*, pp. 6–8.

Questions

1. What do you understand by the term 'social survey'?
2. Compare and contrast experiments and surveys.

3. Collect a series of newspaper cuttings on 'surveys'. What do these reveal about the characteristics of survey work?

☐ Questionnaire Design

Questionnaire design is central to the success of survey work. In the reading which follows, Walter Borg and Meredith Gall summarise some of the key issues involved in constructing questionnaire items.

Reading 2

1. Clarity is essential; ambiguity must be avoided. If your results are to be valid an item must mean the same thing to all respondents. For example, terms like "several," "most," and "usually" have no precise meaning and should be avoided. In his study of respondents' interpretation of questionnaire items, William Belson obtained 28 different interpretations of the word "usually." Only 60 percent of the interpretations reflected the approximate intent of the investigator.

2. Short items are preferable to long items because short items are easier to understand. Avoid questions that are unnecessarily detailed.

3. Negative items should be avoided as they are misread by many respondents; that is, the negative word is overlooked, resulting in the respondent giving an answer that is opposite to the person's real opinion.

4. Avoid "double-barreled" items, which require the subject to respond to two separate ideas with a single answer. An item such as "Although labor unions are desirable in most fields, they have no place in the teaching profession" cannot be answered with the usual closed-question format (such as strongly agree, agree, no opinion, disagree, strongly disagree) by a person who disagrees with one part of the item and agrees with the other part.

5. Do not use technical terms, jargon, or "big words" that some respondents may not understand. Remember, clarity is especially important in questionnaires since the respondent is usually reached by mail and has no one available to explain unclear items.

6. When a general and a related specific question are to be asked together, it is preferable to ask the general question first. If the specific question is asked first, it tends to narrow the focus of the following general question and to change responses to the general question.

7. Finally, it is very important that an effort be made to avoid biased or leading questions. If the subject is given hints as to the type of answer you would most prefer, there is some tendency to give you what you want. This tendency is especially strong when the letter of transmittal that accompanies the questionnaire has been signed by someone that the subject is eager to please.

W.R. Borg and M.D. Gall (1989), *Educational Research: An Introduction* (5th edition), pp. 430–1.

Questions

1. Examine a questionnaire in any empirical study you have read. Do the questions meet the criteria in the reading?
2. Write a questionnaire item to discover what people understand by 'research methods'. How can you avoid jargon?
3. Write a questionnaire item to discover whether students enjoy taking sociology. How do you avoid bias or writing a leading question?

☐ Survey Interviews

Much has been written about the ways in which researchers conduct interviews in social research. In the reading which follows some of the characteristics of the survey interview are discussed.

Reading 3

Interviewers are trained for their role in an interview. Respondents are not. They need assistance and reassurance in the unfamiliar task they have been asked to perform.

The respondent has to realize that he is taking part neither in an oral examination, nor in an ordinary conversation; if he thinks he is being tested, he may worry that he may give a 'wrong' answer or that he is unqualified to answer certain questions; if he thinks the interview is a friendly chat, he may stray from the subject or try to answer the wrong questions.

Interviewers have to maintain a detached attitude, but ensure that the interview is relaxed and friendly. It is helpful if the interviewer looks at the respondent often, especially just after asking a question, to pick up and deal with signs of worry and bewilderment immediately and to take simple steps to promote informality and co-operation. Too little eye contact may make the interviewer appear uninterested and withdrawn; too much, however, can be embarrassing for the respondent.

Playing a constructive role

The respondent's interest and good will has to be maintained throughout an interview. The interviewer has to ensure, for example, that the pace of the interview suits the respondent. Some people answer quickly and want to get on with the interview as fast as possible. Others need more time to think; the respondent is, after all, hearing the questions for the first time and may be considering ideas that have not occurred to him before.

Whereas in introducing themselves and gaining respondents' co-operation interviewers are generally encouraged to use their own words, in asking the questions they must always use the precise words printed on the questionnaire. Even apparently trivial changes in wording can affect the respondent's perceptions of what is being asked and thus affect his answers.

If a respondent seems to have misunderstood or misinterpreted a question the first time he hears it, it should be repeated slowly. The interviewer should not try to explain it in different words, as these might prejudice the reply. If the respondent asks the interviewer what the question means, the interviewer should first try to find out what the respondent thinks it means. If he is right, the interviewer can then tell him so; if he is wrong, he should be guided towards the correct meaning with no deviation from the original wording.

It is often difficult to keep respondents to the point. If a respondent starts to answer one question by giving information that is asked for in a later question, the interviewer will need to stop him with the explanation that the point occurs later. Even if the respondent appears to be giving a full answer to the later question it is best not to make a forward recording. The subsequent question wording may affect the reply, or an intervening question may remind the respondent of another aspect of the subject. Although the sequence should not be altered, intervening phrases such as 'I'd just like to check,' can be inserted when a question is reached that a respondent has attempted to answer earlier. If a respondent wishes to go back to a previous question to change or add to his answer, the interviewer cannot easily refuse. But for consistency, interviewers should be instructed to make a note beside the appropriate question on the questionnaire rather than change the original coding.

Interviewers can and will add informality to the interview by adding link phrases and comments of their own. But it is important that these phrases and comments have no bearing on the answers given and thus cannot bias the results. This should be stressed to interviewers in their basic training.

G. Hoinville, R. Jowell and associates (1978), *Survey Research Practice*, pp. 98–9.

Questions

1. What are the characteristics of the survey interview?
2. Given the description of the interview, what are the implications for the interviewer's role?
3. What skills do you think you require to conduct survey interviews?

☐ The Interview Schedule

Preparing for an interview requires a clear interview schedule which includes an introduction to the survey and a set of questions and prompt cards. The reading by Rosemarie Newell describes the format of an interview schedule.

Reading 4

The interview schedule, or interview guide, will be handled by a trained interviewer; these documents may be used for face-to-face or telephone interviews. It is important that the same guidelines are followed by each interviewer and, therefore, instructions must be explicit.

Even if the interviewee has received prior notification of the interview by letter or telephone, the interview schedule must begin with a brief introduction, stating who the interviewer is, which organisation he or she represents and the purpose of the interview. Confidentiality and anonymity should be stressed.

Interview schedules, like questionnaires, must provide filter questions to ensure that the interviewer can move smoothly from section to section. This is particularly important in telephone interviewing when silences over the telephone while the interviewer sifts through the questions may confuse or annoy interviewees. Several filter questions and examples of other features of interview schedules are shown in Figure 6.9, an extract from the housing survey.

For some closed questions, it can be more convenient to offer grouped answers on a prompt card (see Figure 6.10). For example, in most instances the exact date of birth of respondents is not of interest, but just their age group. Participants also find it more convenient (and, in terms of age, sometimes less embarrassing) to indicate a range, as shown in Figure 6.10(a). Cards can also be used to list various alternatives from which the interviewee can choose. For example, when asking the questions: 'What are the most important aspects of being employed?', the card can list the responses shown in Figure 6.10(b). Cards can be used for attitude questions. For example, the responses offered for the proposition, 'The government should provide housewives with an income'

IF HOUSEHOLD TOOK UP TENANCY IN 1983 OR LATER (IN LAST 5 YEARS)

ASK SECTION 1, if not, GO TO SECTION 2.

SECTION 1. INITIAL TAKE UP OF TENANCY

1. When you moved into your present house/flat did you move:

From Council Waiting List _____	1 (1)
From temporary Hostel (Homeless) accommodation _	2
Moved because of modernisation programme _____	3
Transfer or exchange of Council property _____	4
Other (Specify) _____	7
NA/NR _____	9

    (a) Is your present house/flat temporary (short-term) accommodation?

Yes – temporary accommodation _____	1 (2)
No – permanent home _____	2
Don't know _____	8
NA/NR _____	9

2. When you first took up the tenancy what was the internal decoration like?

Very good _____	1 (3)
Good _____	2
Acceptable _____	3
Poor _____	4
Very poor _____	5
Don't know _____	8
NA/NR _____	9

    If Poor or 'Very Poor'

    (a) How did you feel about this?

Extremely upset/very disturbed/desperate _____	1 (4)
Very unhappy _____	2
Unhappy _____	3
Did not mind/not concerned _____	4
Quite happy _____	5
NA/NR _____	9

    (b) Did you receive a decoration allowance (because of the poor decorative order of the property)?

Yes _____	1 (5)
No _____	2
Don't know _____	8
NA/NR _____	9

Figure 6.9 An extract from the Public Housing Survey

might be as shown in Figure 6.10(c). Supplying prompts will also help respondents remember events which they might otherwise have forgotten.

If there is a long list of statements to be read or shown to interviewees, it is possible that items at the top of the list are attended to more closely than those in the middle or at the bottom. To reduce this potential bias, the items in the lists can be rearranged with some interviewers using one order and others using an alternative.

An interviewee cannot look at a card when being interviewed by telephone so an alternative technique is to read all the items and obtain a yes/no answer to each one separately. The number of items will need to be limited to three or four for this to work.

Your Age	financial reward	Strongly agree
18–25	social contact	Agree
26–35	self-esteem	Neither agree nor
36–45	company benefits	disagree
46–55	something to do	Disagree
56 and over	other	Strongly disagree
(a)	(b)	(c)

Figure 6.10 An extract from the Public Housing Survey

R. Newell (1993), 'Questionnaires' in N. Gilbert (ed), *Researching Social Life*, pp. 110–12.

Questions

1. Write an interviewer's introduction for a survey of your choice remembering to include details of
   (a) the organisation you represent;
   (b) details of the survey;
   (c) the importance of the survey;
   (d) confidentiality;
   (e) how long the interview will take.
2. What are 'filter questions'? Give an example.
3. What is a 'prompt card'? Describe the different forms these can take and how they can be used.

☐ The Survey Interviewer

Survey interviewers are trained and employed by companies who specialise in the conduct of social research. Many survey interviewers are female and work on a range of different projects.

Reading 5

Doing Feminist Research
Edited by Helen Roberts

Contributors
Lynne Chisholm, Christine Delphy, Catriona Llewellyn,
David Morgan, Ann Oakley, Joyce Pettigrew,
Helen Roberts, Dale Spender, Diana Woodward

Cover design from H. Roberts (ed), *Doing Feminist Research* (1981).

Questions

1. What does this cartoon tell you about interviewing?
2. What does this cartoon tell you about interviewers? Is a stereotype
   involved?
3. What kind of training do you think interviewers require?

□ Postal Surveys

As well as surveys being conducted through face-to-face interviews, they are also conducted using postal questionnaires. Often the size of the sample and questions of cost influence the decision to use postal questionnaires. This reading outlines the conduct of a survey using a postal questionnaire.

Reading 6

A pilot study of victims of domestic accidents was carried out in Bristol in 1974. This pilot study had two major objectives: firstly, to obtain a sample of people who had suffered serious injuries as a result of an accident in the home for the purpose of pretesting questions concerning the consequences of the accident for the victim and his or her family; and secondly, to investigate the extent to which victims of such accidents made use of the legal system to obtain damages for their injuries (Genn and Burman, 1977). The study was designed in two parts, the first consisting of a postal questionnaire sent to domestic accident victims and the second part consisting of a personal re-interview of those accident victims who had recorded on their postal questionnaire that they had suffered a serious injury or who had thought that their accident was in any part the fault of another person. The original sample of domestic accident victims was obtained from the Medical Research Division of the Health Education Council (HEC) which conducted its own survey of domestic accidents in one area of Bristol during the years 1970–5. Our sample of names obtained from the HEC consisted of 1234 accidents involving 1214 people. A short postal questionnaire was sent to all victims asking whether the accident they had suffered had resulted in any difficulty in carrying out certain 'key' activities of daily life, and whether they thought that anyone had been wholly or partly to blame for the accident.

The questionnaire was made as simple as possible, requiring respondents to tick boxes or to give simple yes/no answers, and was only one page long. Various measures were taken to ensure as high a response rate as possible. Letters were printed under the Health Education Council's letterhead (already familiar to the sample) and questionnaires were printed on the back of the letter (see Fig. 5.1). Each letter was signed individually; good-quality white stationery was used and both the outgoing and the enclosed envelopes were stamped rather than franked. For the initial questionnaire and the second reminder, outgoing envelopes were sent by first-class mail and all envelopes were addressed to named individuals. Two weeks after the original questionnaire had been posted a reminder was sent to non-respondents by second class mail in a stamped envelope, but without a questionnaire; and two weeks later this was followed, where necessary, by a second reminder, backed by a further copy of the original questionnaire.

Of the 1234 questionnaires mailed, 871 (70·6 per cent) elicited some response, and 811 (65·7 per cent) were adequately completed (Genn and Burman, 1976). Of the 871 questionnaires returned, 56 per cent were received in the first twelve day period after mailing; a further 22 per cent were received after the first reminder letter was sent out and the same proportion was

---

The
Health
Education
Council

Medical Research Division
Canynge Hall
Whiteladies Road
Bristol BS8 2PR
0272-38255

Dear Sir or Madam,

    As you will remember, we visited you about a year ago, shortly after an accident in your home. You helped us at that time by telling us about the accident and how it was caused.

    We are now working with the Centre for Socio-Legal Studies in Oxford, and with them are looking at what happened in the weeks which followed. We are interested in two things — first of all, in how injuries from the accident affected daily life, and secondly, whether you considered claiming legal compensation for any losses.

    It would be very helpful for our work if you would answer the questions on the back of this letter, and return it to us in the enclosed envelope. We are anxious to have replies from everyone, even if the accident had no effect on your daily life.

    If the person who had the accident is too young to answer the questions, would a parent or other adult please answer for him or her. If you have any questions about this letter, Mrs Heather Whicher will be happy to answer them between 9.30—12.00 noon Mondays to Fridays; her telephone number is Bristol 38255.

    The information you give us will of course be treated as confidential, as in the past.

    Thank you once again for your help.

Yours faithfully,

On behalf of Dr. John Dale,
Director of Medical Research

Figure 5.1

Figure 5.1 – (Cont'd)

CONFIDENTIAL

A.

Did your accident result in any injury which made it difficult or impossible for you to do any of the following things as you normally would? If so, please put a tick ☑ in one of the right-hand columns to show how long it lasted.

	For less than 1 week	For 1–3 weeks	For more than 3 weeks
1. Look after yourself e.g. wash or dress yourself	☐	☐	☐
2. Move about in the house and out of doors	☐	☐	☐
3. Do housework	☐	☐	☐
4. Carry on with your work or job as usual	☐	☐	☐

For children

6. Go to school & take part in all school activities	☐	☐	☐
7. Get around and play as usual	☐	☐	☐
8. Look after himself or herself as usual	☐	☐	☐

IF THE ACCIDENT CAUSED NONE OF THESE DIFFICULTIES, PLEASE WRITE NO HERE ....

B. Did you think that someone else was to blame (even only partly) for your accident? Please read the list below and put a tick ☑ against any which apply.

☐ a shop or manufacturer
☐ a workman, such as a builder or plumber
☐ a local council
☐ a landlord
☐ a neighbour
☐ someone else in the family
☐ any other person (please write in) ....
☐ only my fault
☐ no one's fault

C. Did you consider making a legal claim for money to compensate for your injuries? (Do not include claims for Social Security benefits.)

Please write in YES or NO ....

D. Did you get advice about a legal claim from anyone? Please read the list below and put a ☑ against any which apply to you.

☐ a solicitor
☐ the police
☐ a trade union
☐ an employer
☐ Citizen's Advice Bureau
☐ a friend or relative
☐ someone else (please write in) ....

received in the final period following a further reminder together with a new questionnaire. The last questionnaires which were returned arrived 2¹/₂ months after the initial mailing.

The overall response rate to this postal questionnaire must be considered in relation to the fact that the sample surveyed had already been part of a previous study by a different organisation and was homogeneous in that members had all suffered a domestic accident of some kind during the previous 18 months.

M. Maclean and H. Genn (1979), *Methodological Issues in Social Surveys*, pp. 80–2.

Questions

1. How did the researchers attempt to persuade respondents to answer the questionnaire?
2. Write a letter for a postal survey on a topic of your choice.
3. Design a postal questionnaire containing only four questions on the topic you chose above. What problems were involved in designing the questions?

☐ Coding

The responses provided in social surveys are often handled by computer analysis. As a result, the responses need to be converted into numbers which are called codes. In this reading the process of coding is outlined.

Reading 7

Codes can be allocated either before the question is answered (precoding) or afterwards (postcoding).

Precoding

With forced-choice questions it is possible to allocate codes to answers before people fill in the questionnaire since we have determined beforehand what range of answers we will get. To make it easier to code someone's actual responses, the codes that represent each answer are printed on the questionnaire itself.

This can be done in different ways (Figure 14.1).

Figure 14.1 Two methods of precoding questions

Are you:	1 ☐ Married	Are you:	1 Married
(tick box)	2 ☐ Never married	(circle number)	2 Never married
	3 ☐ Separated		3 Separated
	4 ☐ Divorced		4 Divorced
	5 ☐ Widowed		5 Widowed
	6 ☐ Other		6 Other

Postcoding
With open-ended questions coding cannot be done until after the questions have actually been answered. There are two main approaches to this process of postcoding.

1 A pre-established coding scheme can be used. Where we have a good idea of how we want to code answers, we simply code according to this scheme. An example is in coding occupation. Actual occupations may be put into broad, pre-established categories such as professional, managerial, clerical, trade, semi-skilled and so forth. A rule of thumb when coding in this way is to retain a fair amount of detail in this coding. For example, instead of coding occupation as simply white-collar and blue-collar we might code reasonably specific occupations (e.g. teacher, plumber) or at least broad occupational categories (e.g. upper professional, farmer on large farm, skilled trade). These fairly specific codes can be collapsed into less specific categories later on. The reverse is not possible: you cannot create specific categories if the original coding does not include the detail.

2 Develop a set of coding categories on the basis of people's answers to the questions. That is, let the coding categories emerge from the data instead of imposing them on the data. For example, we may have asked 'What do you think of the government's immigration policy?' To develop a set of codes go through the first 50 to 100 responses, make a list of people's answers and see if they can be grouped under various headings. Some answers might be classified as approving and others as disapproving. Of the disapproving answers it might be worthwhile developing various categories such as 'unhappy because too few migrants are allowed in', or 'because too many are admitted'; others may reflect dissatisfaction with the criteria for admission or with the countries from which migrants come. When we have developed a set of categories such that all

responses can be slotted in somewhere, each category is given a code and each person's response coded. Make sure that all the categories are mutually exclusive: a person has to be coded into only one category per variable. Where someone fits into several categories either decide which one is to take precedence for coding purposes or develop a separate code which covers that particular response.

Coding numerical data
For some variables such as age, income, number of children and so on, people's answers are already in numerical form so it is not necessary to convert the answer into a code. We can simply code their exact answer. Thus if someone is 39 years old we would simply give them the code 39. Often people are asked to tick a particular income or age category (e.g. 25–35; 36–45). In these cases it is best to give people a code which represents the midpoint of the category. Thus for someone in the category 36–45 we would code them as 40. Where people are asked to respond in this way it is worth putting the mid-point next to each category to make the coding easier later on.

D.A. de Vaus (1986), *Surveys in Social Research*, pp. 187–9.

Questions

1. What do you understand by 'precoding'?
2. What is 'postcoding'?
3. Which method of precoding in the reading do you prefer? Give reasons for your answer.

Project Questions

1. Design a questionnaire using open and closed questions on food choice among the students in your year group.
2. Use the questionnaire you have designed to interview some students in your year. What problems are involved in conducting such interviews? How could they be overcome?
3. Establish a set of codes for the questions in your study. Compare and contrast the issues involved in coding open and closed questions.

Further Reading

J. Bell, *Doing Your Research Project* (Open University Press, 1987), contains useful guidance on survey research (see, especially, the checklists).

M. Bulmer (ed), *Sociological Research Methods* (Macmillan, 1984; 2nd edition), contains a useful section devoted to survey research.

D.A. de Vaus, *Surveys in Social Research* (Allen and Unwin, 1986; printed in a new edition by UCL Press), is a clear practical guide to survey investigation.

N. Gilbert (ed), *Researching Social Life* (Sage, 1993), contains several chapters on designing, conducting and analysing surveys.

G. Hoinville, R. Jowell and Associates, *Survey Research Practice* (Heinemann, 1978), discusses ways in which to organise surveys.

E. Kane, *Doing Your Own Research* (Marion Boyars, 1985), contains a useful chapter on questionnaires.

C. Marsh, *The Survey Method* (Allen and Unwin, 1982), is a classic defence of the social survey.

P. McNeill, *Research Methods* (Routledge, 1990; 2nd edition), contains a very readable chapter on social surveys suitable for student use.

6 | Doing ethnography

Traditionally, ethnographic studies have been associated with the work of social anthropologists who visited societies other than their own for the purposes of academic study. In these circumstances, ethnographic work involved the ethnographer living in the social situation that was to be studied. The methods of investigation that were used, therefore, included observation and participant observation, unstructured and informal interviewing and, where appropriate, some documentary evidence.

In recent years, anthropologists have not only studied other societies, but also used this approach to study their own societies in general and urban settings in particular. In turn, sociologists have also used an ethnographic approach to study schools, hospitals, factories and a range of other social organisations.

Common to all this work has been the method of participant observation where the main instrument of social investigation has been the researcher who enters into the daily life of those who are being studied. Such a situation involves watching the people in the group and the way they behave. However, the researcher also enters into conversation with the people who are being studied in order to get their perceptions of the events and situations that are being studied. The researcher then makes a record of these events in order to analyse the social situation.

Each person who engages in an ethnographic study therefore needs to acquire a range of skills. First, the researcher needs to be able to engage in a social situation by living among the people who are to be studied. Secondly, the language (including any special terminology) needs to be acquired. Thirdly, the researcher needs not only to be able to observe, but also to conduct interviews. Finally, part of the business of doing ethnographic work is to be able to record and analyse what occurs in social situations.

Ethnographers take roles in social situations. However, it is important to recall that the ascribed characteristics of the researcher influence the role that can be taken. In this respect, the age, gender and ethnicity of the researcher influences the role that can be played.

Many commentators have subdivided the role of the participant observer into formal and informal and passive and active. In many situations, these roles are portrayed as being part of a continuum with a passive role being at one end of the continuum and an active role at the other. Further subdivisions of participant observation have been identified through a fourfold classification of complete participant, participant as observer, observer as participant and complete observer. Each of these roles involves certain characteristics which influence the way the research is conducted.

The 'complete participant' becomes a member of a group but does not tell the people that they are being studied. The result is that the researcher plays a covert role. While this allows the researcher to collect observational data, it also raises several problems given that the researcher does not declare a research intention. Secondly, there is difficulty in being able to follow up research topics as the study is undeclared. Nevertheless, such an approach is often justified on the grounds that it overcomes the problem that researchers have in gaining access to difficult social situations, but we might still ask what the difference is between such an approach and spying.

In contrast, the 'participant as observer' presents the research that is being done, participates in a social setting and takes a particular role. The focus of such a research role is the relationship between the researcher and the researched – a situation that requires considerable understanding on the part of the researcher. Other roles that are not so frequently used include the 'observer-as-participant' role where the observation of the group under study is made public from the beginning of the project. Finally, there is the 'complete observer' role which may be easy to identify in the abstract, but difficult to handle in social situations. Such a role suggests that the researcher conducts observations with minimal social interaction – a situation that is difficult to achieve in a pure form.

However, it is important to appreciate that such roles emphasise 'ideal type' situations. In practice, participant observers find that they have to take on a range of roles that relate to the social situation that is being studied. The result is that the role of participant observer changes over time during the course of a research project.

There are a number of issues that all those who engage in ethnographic studies and conduct participant observation need to consider. They include:

1 The extent to which the participant observer influences the social situation in which the research occurs. Such factors as age, sex, social class and ethnicity are important in this context.

2 The extent to which a project is to be overt or covert. While this is a major choice, a project is rarely either totally overt or totally covert. Accordingly, researchers need to monitor their activities carefully.

3 The extent to which personal characteristics influence the roles that are taken, the relationships that are established and the data that are obtained.

4 The way in which participant observation relates to other methods of data collection.

5 The role that the participant observer has not only to participate in a social setting, but also to record, analyse and write about the social setting.

In short, doing ethnography and being a participant observer demands a range of social and academic skills that can be used to generate data and understand a range of social settings.

□ The Rationale for Ethnography

What are the characteristics of ethnographic research? Many investigators present ethnography as an approach that overcomes problems associated with quantitative research. In this reading, Martyn Hammersley outlines the criticisms made of quantitative work before turning to the way in which it is argued that qualitative research (especially ethnography) overcomes these problems.

Reading 1

The rationale for ethnography is based on a critique of quantitative, notably survey and experimental, research. The validity of this research is challenged on a number of grounds:

    1 that the structured character of the data collection process involves the imposition of the researcher's assumptions about the social world and consequently reduces the chances of discovering evidence discrepant with those assumptions.

2   that making claims about what happens in 'natural' settings on the basis of data produced in settings that have been specially set up by the researcher – whether experiment or formal interview – is to engage in a largely implicit and highly questionable form of generalisation.

3   that to rely on what people *say* about what they believe and do, without also *observing* what they do, is to neglect the complex relationship between attitudes and behaviour; just as to rely on observation without also talking with people in order to understand their perspectives is to risk misinterpreting their behaviour.

4   that quantitative analysis reifies social phenomena by treating them as more clearly defined and distinct than they are, and by neglecting the processes by which they develop and change.

5   that quantitative analysis assumes that people's actions are the mechanical products of psychological and social factors, thereby neglecting the creative role of individual cognition and group interaction.

This is not an exhaustive list of the criticisms directed at quantitative research by ethnographers, but it reveals the main assumptions underlying advocacy of qualitative method: that the nature of the social world must be *discovered*; that this can only be achieved by first-hand observation and participation in 'natural' settings, guided by an exploratory orientation; that accounts of the findings of such research must capture the processes involved and the social meanings that generate them. On the basis of these assumptions, ethnography is directed towards producing what are referred to as 'theoretical', 'analytical' or 'thick' descriptions (whether of societies, small communities, organisations, spatial locations, or social worlds'). These descriptions must remain close to the concrete reality of particular events but at the same time reveal general features of human social life.

M. Hammersley (1990), 'What's Wrong With Ethnography? The myths of theoretical description', *Sociology*, Vol. 24, No. 4, pp. 597–8.

Questions

1. Using Martyn Hammersley's list outlining the grounds for challenging quantitative work, suggest what the characteristics of qualitative work might be.

2. How can the social researcher discover the social world? Illustrate your answer by reference to the social world of:
    (a) schools or colleges
    (b) hospitals

(c) public libraries
(d) cinemas.
3. Why do you think Martyn Hammersley considers ethnography to be 'theoretical', 'analytical' or 'thick' description? Give reasons for your answer.

☐ Developing Roles in Participant Observation

The main method of social investigation used by the ethnographer is participant observation in which the researcher develops a role. In this reading, I demonstrate how participant observers need to develop several roles during the same investigation.

Reading 2

Research roles are constantly negotiated and renegotiated with different informants throughout a research project (cf. Schatzman and Strauss, 1973). In my own study I found that although I principally took a participant-as-observer role there were several different phases associated with this role over time and which varied with the individuals with whom I worked. As far as phases of the research role were concerned I found that I was in different phases with different individuals. Accordingly, Table 4.1 [see p. 82] summarises the phases of my role relationship with three individuals with whom I was in daily contact during the first six months of my research project in Bishop McGregor School (Burgess, 1983). First, Sylvia Robinson who was Head of the Newsom Department during my first term in the school. Secondly, Roy Carey, the Head of the Mathematics Department who was a member of the House to which I belonged and, finally, Mrs Watson the School Secretary.

These three examples indicate the complexity involved in a research situation where the researcher may be simultaneously perceived in different terms by different members of the same institution. These three cases have been presented as they show how my role went through different phases during the same period of my research. In these terms, the literature oversimplifies the situation as it tends to be assumed that the researcher simultaneously goes through similar phases with all members of the situation studied. An ideal type of situation is presented rather than an actual situation.

R.G. Burgess (1984), *In The Field: An Introduction to Field Research*, pp. 85, 87, 88.

Table 4.1 Phases in the development of research roles with three informants at Bishop McGregor School

	Newcomer	Provisional acceptance	Categorical acceptance	Personal acceptance	Imminent migrant
Sylvia Robinson	Sylvia introduces me to staff as 'Mr Burgess who has come to work with our Newsom pupils'. (1.5.73)	Concerned that I might not have enough to do – attempts to get me into other classes so that I can teach and do research. (3.5.73)	Sylvia says that she sees me as a teacher who can teach Newsom classes and take substitution lessons. (22.5.73)	Sees me as a member of staff. (5.6.73) Offers to lend me her car. (25.9.73)	Concerned that if I was to leave the school it would leave a gap in the Newsom timetable. (18.9.73)
Roy Carey	Perceives me as a visitor. (3.5.73) Perceives me as a visitor. (3.7.73)				
Mrs Watson (School Secretary)	Secretary refuses to allow me access to office files – she is uncertain about my role. (8.5.73)	Allows access to files only when she has checked with the Head – she has had some clarification of my role. (22.5.73)	Allows me to use office files and jokes with me. (6.9.73)	Secretary says she thinks of me as one of the staff. (4.10.73)	

Note: The dates associated with the various phases of my role were obtained from field notes.

Questions

1. What do you understand by the term 'negotiating and renegotiating' research roles?
2. Compare and contrast the roles I took with the three people listed on the table. Suggest reasons for the different roles.
3. What roles could you take in studying your school or college? How would you establish your role with
   (a) a school or college secretary
   (b) a teacher who you do not know?

☐ Ascribed Roles and the Researcher

Much of the literature concerning ethnography focuses on the roles which are developed by the participant observer, yet the ascribed roles of the researcher: age, sex and ethnicity, can influence field relations. Three short extracts make up this reading to illustrate the impact these ascribed characteristics have on research.

Reading 3

Gary Alan Fine and Kent Sandstrom focus on age when doing participant observation with children and young people.

Problems of access and trust stem not only from the children's suspicions of participant observers. Adult authority figures may also pose challenges when they attempt to use participant observers for their own ends – not necessarily cynically, of course. Birksted (1976) found that his observation in a school served a useful purpose for the school in that it kept students busy and, in some measure, out of trouble. Yet, he was unable to meet the school's expectations of an adult:

> Since I persisted in spending most of my time with pupils I was only accepted by a few members of the staff. I avoided teaching, and the one class I was pushed into taking ended by complaints about noise from the teacher next door [Birksted, 1976, p. 66].

The senior author felt similar pressures when asked to run practices, umpire, and once to coach a team when its regular coaches had to be out of town. At several times during the research, he was asked for advice about children with minor behavior problems. Although desiring to help, he felt unable to divulge any information.

G.A. Fine and K.L. Sandstrom (1988), *Knowing Children, Participant Observation with Minors*, p. 29.

Janet Foster conducted an ethnographic study of petty crime called *Villains*. Here she explains how being a women influenced her work.

One of the questions which is always asked of participant observers is *how* they got in. Like other research of this kind, access for me came about as a result of a chance meeting with Chris. She offered to introduce me to some of her friends who had offended in their youth and socialised in the Grafton Arms, but suggested that the nature of my research should remain covert. I was therefore introduced as Janet, who was a student, and wanted to join the ladies' darts team. Here began the first of many learning experiences (since I had never played darts!) and the first of several ethical dilemmas. I began by visiting the Grafton on ladies' darts night and within a short time was a regular in the pub most evenings of the week. The darts provided me with an excellent opportunity to mix with the men and gave me a 'legitimate' reason for being there. As I was keen to learn they all took a great deal of time and patience (with my appalling subtraction!) helping me.

I never made any attempt to speak or dress differently, and my accent presented few problems. One person described me as 'working class with a nice accent!', while others explained it as a product of my roots. George, for example, defended me when one of her 'mates' commented, 'Your friend's a bit posh, ain't she?' George replied, 'Janet comes from Bournemouth and they all speak like that down there!'

Being small, young, and female was a decided advantage in negotiating most aspects of the field. People always responded to me primarily as a woman and secondarily as a student who was doing a 'project' or writing a book – a task which was not viewed very seriously.

J. Foster (1990), *Villains: Crime and Community in the Inner City*, pp. 167–8.

Elliot Liebow examines the role of ethnicity in his study of street-corner men.

Throughout this period, my field observations were focused on individuals: what they said, what they did, and the contexts in which they said them or did them. I sought them out and was sought out by them.

My field notes contain a record of what I saw when I looked at Tally, Richard, Sea Cat and the others. I have only a small notion – and one that I myself consider suspect – of what they saw when they looked at me.

Some things, however, are very clear. They saw, first of all, a white man. In my opinion, this brute fact of color, as they understood it in their experience and as I understood it in mine, irrevocably and absolutely relegated me to the status of outsider. I am not certain, but I have a hunch that they were more continuously aware of the color difference than I was. When four of us sat around a kitchen table, for example, I saw three Negroes; each of them saw two Negroes and a white man.

Whenever the fact of my being white was openly introduced, it pointed up the distance between me and the other person, even when the intent of introducing it was, I believe, to narrow that distance.

E. Liebow (1967), *Tally's Corner*, pp. 248–9.

Questions

1. Consider how age might assist or impede an ethnographic study of primary school pupils in your locality.
2. In what ways did the female role assist Janet Foster's fieldwork? What might be the implications for other work?
3. What barriers are there to conducting ethnographic studies? How might status and social distance be reduced by a researcher?

☐ Working with a Key Informant

A classic ethnographic study based on participant observation is William Foote Whyte's *Street Corner Society*. Whyte was assisted in his research by an informant he called 'Doc' whose role in the study is discussed in this reading.

Reading 4

I learned early in my Cornerville period the crucial importance of having the support of the key individuals in any groups or organizations I was studying. Instead of trying to explain myself to everyone, I found I was providing far more information about myself and my study to leaders such as Doc than I volunteered to the average corner boy. I always tried to give the impression that I was willing and eager to tell just as much about my study as anyone wished to know, but it was only with group leaders that I made a particular effort to provide really full information.

My relationship with Doc changed rapidly in this early Cornerville period. At first he was simply a key informant – and also my sponsor. As we spent more time together, I ceased to treat him as a passive informant. I discussed with him quite frankly what I was trying to do, what problems were puzzling me, and so on. Much of our time was spent in this discussion of ideas and observations, so that Doc became, in a very real sense, a collaborator in the research.

This full awareness of the nature of my study stimulated Doc to look for and point out to me the sorts of observations that I was interested in. Often when I picked him up at the flat where he lived with his sister and brother-in-law, he said to me: "Bill, you should have been around last night. You would have been interested in this." And then he would go on to tell me what had happened. Such accounts were always interesting and relevant to my study.

Doc found this experience of working with me interesting and enjoyable, and yet the relationship had its drawbacks. He once commented: "You've slowed me up plenty since you've been down here. Now, when I do something, I have to think what Bill Whyte would want to know about it and how I can explain it. Before, I used to do things by instinct."

However, Doc did not seem to consider this a serious handicap. Actually, without any training he was such a perceptive observer that it only needed a little stimulus to help him to make explicit much of the dynamics of the social organization of Cornerville. Some of the interpretations I have made are his more than mine, although it is now impossible to disentangle them.

While I worked more closely with Doc than with any other individual, I always sought out the leader in whatever group I was studying. I wanted not only sponsorship from him but also more active collaboration with the study. Since these leaders had the sort of position in the community that enabled them to observe much better than the followers what was going on and since they were in general more skilful observers than the followers, I found that I had much to learn from a more active collaboration with them.

W.F. Whyte (1981), *Street Corner Society* (3rd edition), pp. 300–2.

Questions

1. What did Whyte learn from his relationship with Doc?
2. List the different roles that Doc played in Whyte's study and assess his significance on the study.
3. In what ways might an informant's involvement in a study lead to bias? How could this be overcome?

☐ Interviewing in Ethnographic Studies

Although ethnographic studies rely heavily on observation and participant observation, it is also essential for the researcher to use other methods of investigation. Many researchers conduct conversations and interviews in their studies as Barry Cocklin indicates in this reading.

Reading 5

During the process of participant observation, there were a number of situations in which a one-to-one discussion occurred ranging along a continuum from taped, single topic sessions to informal 'chats'. However, these are considered an integral part of the interactive processes of participant observation and distinguished from the 'semi-structured' form termed 'interviews' conducted with the adult students at the end of each term and on two occasions with members of the school staff.

In both contexts, the intention was to obtain a summary of the experiences utilizing some 'key questions' suggested by an examination of the data. However, these interviews remained 'semi-structured' in that the replies by respondents led to the generation of further questions as I sought explanations and elaboration of the events.

At the start of each interview, I reiterated their 'voluntary participation', noted the use of the tape recorder as a tool to aid recall of the conversation, and that all comments would be transcribed under their code number. This, then, represented part of the processes of renegotiation of access and consent and was then followed by an indication of the general purpose and 'agenda' of the interview (Burgess, 1984). The interviews (see Ives, 1974) ranged in time between 30 minutes and 1.5 hours, with most occupying the hour. The format varied from very free-flowing open discussions to the 'hesitant', question/answer sessions with the only adult student to repeatedly report his 'unease' in the interview situation which, as noted previously, related to the formal use of the tape recorder. Overall, however, these interviews were 'open', 'wide ranging' and led to the gathering of considerable information.

The interviews with staff were also 'semi-structured' by using a series of general questions to provide some direction to the discussion and to elicit particular information. These questions, however, provided only a basis for the interview, and staff members were informed that an 'informal chat' covering their experiences with, and of, adult students was the preferred 'mode' of the discussion rather than a 'formal, question-based' format (see Simons, 1981). Their co-operation in the use of the recorder was sought and they were informed of the voluntary nature of participation and of the transcription of all their comments, both in this situation and on other occasions, under a code number. I approached each individual staff member to arrange a convenient time for the interview which generally occupied an hour. Two such interviews were held coinciding with the times when the adult students were taking examinations, while a number of less formal conversations were held with staff members when we encountered each other around the school corridors or staffroom.

B. Cocklin (1992), 'Field Research in Schools: Issues of Method and Ethics' in T.J. Lovat (ed), *Sociology for Teachers*, pp. 308–9.

Questions

1. What do you consider to be the role of semi-structured interviews and 'chats' in ethnographic studies? Give reasons for your answer.
2. What can be learned about the use of tape recorders from Barry Cocklin's experiences?
3. Consider when you would use formal interviews, semi-structured interviews and 'chats' in an ethnographic study of your school or college. Give reasons for your choices.

☐ Using an Informant's Diary

Another approach to ethnographic work is through the use of an informant's diary where the researcher encourages those who are being studied to keep a diary for short periods of time. Such diaries may be subsequently used with interviews to obtain further data. In this reading, I describe the use of informants' diaries in school studies.

Reading 6

Ethnographic research involves the study of people *in situ*. It involves the study of informants, their actions and their activities as they occur. Such an approach presupposes that the researcher can gain access to informants and their activities. However, it is evident that in a situation such as a school it is impossible for the researcher to observe all the activities that occur. This arises for a number of reasons. Firstly, the size of the school prevents the researcher being present at all locations. The researcher has to select which classrooms to enter and what groups to study. Secondly, there are some situations that the researcher may not be allowed to directly observe, such as meetings restricted to high status members of the institution, meetings in the head teacher's study and activities in particular classrooms. Finally, a researcher might be denied access to some classrooms when teachers are concerned that their work will be judged or evaluated during the course of the research.

In these circumstances, the researcher needs to obtain accounts from the participants which will yield a further series of observations and first hand accounts. Researchers might, therefore, ask informants to keep diaries about what they do on particular days and in particular lessons. Teachers and pupils could be asked to record the activities in which they engage and the people with whom they interact. In short, what they do (and do not do) in particular social situations. In these circumstances, subjects of the research become more than observers and informants; they are co-researchers as they keep chronological records of their activities.

The diarists (whether they are teachers or pupils) will need to be given a series of instructions to write a diary. These might take the form of notes and suggestions for keeping a continuous record that answers the questions: When? Where? What? Who? Such questions help to focus down the observations that can be recorded. Meanwhile, a diary may be subdivided into chronological periods within the day so that records may be kept for the morning, the afternoon and the evening. Further subdivisions can be made in respect of diaries directed towards activities that occur within the school and classroom. Here, the day may be subdivided into the divisions of the formal timetable with morning, afternoon and lunch breaks. Indeed, within traditional thirty-five or forty minute lessons further subdivisions can be made in respect of the activities that occur within particular time zones (cf. Flanders interaction analysis).

Using informants' diaries gives further detailed data. Firstly, these diaries provide first hand accounts of situations to which the researcher may not have direct access. Secondly, they provide 'insider' accounts of situations. Finally, they provide further sampling of informants, of activities and of time which may complement the observations made by the researcher.

R.G. Burgess (1981), 'Keeping a Research Diary', *Cambridge Journal of Education*, Vol. 11, No. 1, pp. 78–9.

Questions

1. In what circumstances in the study of a school or college might it be appropriate to use informants' diaries?
2. To what extent do you agree or disagree with my analysis of the advantages of informants' diaries? Give reasons for your answer.
3. Design a set of instructions for informants to keep diaries over a two week period of study in your school or college.

Project Questions

1. Outline an observational project that can be conducted in your locality and suggest the role(s) that you can take.
2. Conduct a series of observations in a range of settings using different roles. Summarise what you discover about the characteristics of each role.
3. Conduct an ethnographic study in your school/college over five weeks. Write about:
   (a) the research problem
   (b) the principles of selection involved
   (c) the methods of investigation used
   (d) the data and how they are recorded and analysed.

Further Reading

R.G. Burgess (ed), *Field Research: A Sourcebook and Field Manual* (Allen and Unwin, 1982; now published by Routledge), provides a comprehensive range of papers on the conduct of ethnography.

R.G. Burgess, *In The Field: An Introduction to Field Research* (Allen and Unwin, 1984; now published by Routledge).

M. Hammersley and P. Atkinson, *Ethnography: Principles into Practice* (Tavistock, 1983).

These are major textbooks that contain numerous examples from actual projects.

R. Yin, *Case Study Research* (Sage, 1984), contains an outline of the way in which case study research can be conducted.

Examples of ethnographic research can be found in a range of settings including:

R.G. Burgess, *Experiencing Comprehensive Education: A Study of Bishop McGregor School* (Methuen, 1983), about a comprehensive school at work.

J. Foster, *Villains* (Routledge, 1990), about petty crime.

J. Hockey, *Squaddies* (Exeter University Press, 1985), about regular soldiers.

C. Hughes, *Stepfamilies – Wicked or Wonderful?* (Gower, 1991), about four stepfamilies.

C.J. Pole, *Assessing and Recording Achievement* (Open University Press, 1993), about the introduction of records of achievement in a school.

W.F. Whyte, *Street Corner Society* (University of Chicago Press, 1981; 3rd edition), about streetcorner gangs – the classic study.

7 | Collecting historical accounts

For many years questions have been posed about the similarities and differences between history and sociology. While some researchers would claim a distinction between these areas of study, others would argue that they have much in common, especially in terms of methods used and the problems that researchers confront when collecting historical accounts using personal documents. This chapter, therefore, focuses on some of the main issues and problems involved in the use of personal documents by historians and sociologists. Among issues that we need to consider are: what is the value of documentary and historical materials in sociological studies? What problems are involved in conducting such research and how are they handled?

However, we need to begin by considering what constitutes a documentary source. For some writers working from the historical tradition the word 'document' is restricted to written materials. Yet this places a very narrow definition on documentary evidence and puts the emphasis on official records and personal documents that are obtained from individuals writing from a middle or upper-class perspective. Indeed, as Samuel (1975) has remarked, many documentary materials used by historians have been written by individuals who have been running or attempting to run other people's lives. As a consequence, much of the research work that uses this material is written from a particular perspective whereby the lives of many men and especially women are hidden from view. Indeed, it is only in recent years that women's history has offered a different perspective on the past.

If we are to find out about the lives of people from different social classes, we need to take documents to include written and oral sources. Among the written materials we might include are autobiographies and diaries based on an individual's first hand involvement with a situation. It is personal documents such as these that many researchers argue can help sociologists to obtain an historical understanding of a person, group or situation and block a gap that all too frequently appears in studies based on contemporary events. It is this kind of evidence that sociologists can use to establish hypotheses and test out conceptual schemes in their studies.

Yet some people might claim that personal documents are inherently problematic as, they argue, only those people who are literate write autobiographies and keep diaries. As a consequence, some self-selection is involved and a partial account results. How, we might ask, can researchers deal with these issues? The historian George Kitson Clark has argued that all documents must be the subject of constant critical enquiry. Furthermore, it is argued that questions about the structure and content of documentary materials must be continually posed by the researcher using such sources. Many of the questions that can be raised about documentary materials are similar to those that have to be addressed by researchers working with other methods of social investigation. In this respect, researchers need to consider the questions that should be asked about written documents if issues concerning the reliability and validity of data derived from written sources are to be addressed.

However, written materials are only one kind of documentary source and, as Paul Thompson argues, can provide a partial view of the social world. Accordingly, in recent years, many investigators have started to consider how oral historical materials can be collected, analysed and used alongside written materials. In particular, they focus on those elements of culture that do not automatically lend themselves to written sources but are often transmitted by word of mouth. In rural areas of Eastern England, for example, George Ewart Evans recorded the words of workers who were skilled in crafts associated with working on the land, such as laying hedges and digging ditches. It would be unusual to find a written source on how to perform these tasks and, therefore, oral recording becomes essential.

One approach that brings together written and oral documents is the 'life history' approach that Plummer (1983) has argued is 'the cornerstone of social science life document research'. It usually takes the form of a book length study of an individual's life told in his or her own words. Here, the social scientist collects the material by meeting the individual and writing down or tape recording material that relates to particular periods of his or her life. Often the researcher will want to observe the individual, talk to his or her acquaintances and friends and collect letters and photographs that they possess. But how do researchers begin to explain to individuals what they want to do? Researchers often write to those they wish to interview indicating the kinds of materials that are required. Such letters can highlight the advantages of life history study for informants. Meanwhile, the strengths of life history documents for sociologists were well put by Thomas and Znanecki over sixty years ago in their pioneering study entitled *The Polish Peasant in Europe and America.* These writers did not merely see life histories as useful for sociological research, but regarded them as 'perfect material'. Such a strong claim has resulted in a range of criticisms being made of this approach in terms of representativeness, validity and objectivity. Nevertheless, many researchers consider life histories have great value in presenting personal experience and personal meanings associated with people's lives.

But we might ask: how can such material be used in sociological studies? How can the researcher analyse and interpret documentary sources? This issue has been addressed by June Purvis who argues that historians and sociologists can provide different kinds of analyses which can complement each other in their studies.

Throughout this chapter, we consider different ways in which personal documentary sources can be used alongside each other. Such an approach is not only important in data collection, but also in data analysis. Furthermore, historical and documentary materials need to be used alongside other approaches in the conduct of investigations if this approach is to be integrated into the process of social research.

☐ The Uses of Personal Documents

In an urban industrial society individuals produce and receive a variety of personal documents that contain perspectives on the ways in which they live their lives. Such documents may include written, audio, and visual materials that provide subjective accounts of the social world. This material can be used as sociological data.

Reading 1

The sociological usefulness of autobiographical and other personal documentary accounts is thus not negligible, even when their limitations are admitted. Indeed they are something more than merely an 'interesting' slice of life, or a 'good read' for sixth-formers, first-year undergraduates and the general public. Robert Angell's six-fold scheme, put forward in 1945, still appears useful as a way of formally stating the purposes which personal documents can fulfil in sociology. They may:

(i)   Serve as a means of securing conceptual 'hunches'.
(ii) Suggest new hypotheses to an investigator who is thinking in terms of an established conceptual scheme.
(iii) Serve as a source from which to select data which seem important in terms of common sense, and to formulate rough hypotheses from these facts.
(iv) Serve in the verification of hypotheses.
(v)   Secure greater historical understanding of how a particular social unit has developed.
(vi) Serve as a means of exposition in the communication of sociological findings.

The autobiographical recollection, as a personal document over the collection of which (unlike the life history) the sociologist has no control, does not serve all these purposes but would seem to be of value in relation to the first three and the fifth. If this is doubted in relation to Durham mining villages, examples can be cited from other areas of sociology than community studies where auto-biographical accounts of high social documentary content and considerable sociological interest provide fascinating source material both in their own right and as a basis for re-analysis and fresh theoretical interpretation.

M. Bulmer (1978), 'Personal Documents as Sociological Data' in M. Bulmer (ed), *Mining and Social Change*, pp. 308–9.

Questions

1. What are 'personal documents'? What are their strengths and limitations as sociological data? Give examples to illustrate your answer.
2. What do you understand by the terms:
   (a) 'conceptual hunches'
   (b) 'verification'
   (c) hypotheses?
3. Collect and examine personal documents associated with any one area of social life. What are the sociological uses of the documents you have collected?

□ Analysing Documents

Researchers may collect written documentary evidence but they also need to consider how it can be used. David Dymond provides a guide to the kinds of questions that historians pose when using historical sources.

Reading 2

A document does not present the historian with straightforward, reproducible 'truth'. Indeed we are doomed to failure if we attempt to write history by stitching together extracts from original sources. At its most basic, a document can only convey someone's *version* of what happened in the past, and it will assuredly mislead anyone who approaches it uncritically and with no sense of its historical context. The historian has a duty to interpret, and find shape in, the past. Therefore he must read and re-read, always pondering on the significance of what he is reading. His main method of analysis is first, to ask questions which are relevant to the evidence and probe for its meaning; and secondly, because the original writers cannot be re-interviewed, to work out as many answers as he can, for himself. His questions will be concerned with both the detail and general character of documents.

The practical historian, whatever his period of study, cannot remain entirely unaware of the science of diplomatic. This has nothing to do with historical figures like Metternich and Kissinger, but is a series of critical techniques for investigating the origins and character of documents – particularly, as the word implies, the official diplomas and charters of the medieval period. The essential point is that questions which a diplomatic historian might ask about a medieval charter should pass through the mind of any historian faced with original evidence. Who wrote it, or at least what kind of person wrote it? When, if only approximately, was it written? Does its physical character, say the handwriting, fit the alleged date? Are some of the statements second-hand and derived from earlier sources? Is it a copy? Or a copy of a copy? Is it a forgery?

Basically the whole process is a logical enquiry into the internal and external consistency of documents. It is not necessarily a process of weeding-out or rejection. For example, forgeries may contain genuine and valuable information; by contrast genuine documents do not necessarily tell the whole truth and are often most revealing about the writer's state of mind, his prejudices, assumptions and priorities.

In practice one of the most valuable applications of diplomatic technique is in identifying the work of early historians and antiquaries. The manuscripts of such people are often unsigned and undated; moreover at a later date they were frequently dispersed, re-arranged, cut up, copied and edited. In every county an enormous task of identification, re-sorting and editing remains to be done. A dramatic recent example is Diarmaid McCulloch's work on the so-called 'Chorography of Suffolk'. This manuscript survey had been written by an unknown person in about 1600, but was unfortunately cut up into several hundred fragments and pasted into many scrapbooks. Later these books were sold and dispersed. The modern editor was able to recognise the fragments by the handwriting and content, and to restore the original text almost completely.

So far as the contents of a document are concerned, a whole succession of questions, general and particular, will arise in the mind of the critical historian as he attempts to 'squeeze' out its meaning. For example:

1 What parts of the document reflect the personality of the writer (his temperament, knowledge or lack of it, his interests, emotions and prejudices)?
2 What parts, if any, are determined by administrative procedures or by the conventions of the period?
3 How far is the document apparently based on firsthand experience; or derived at second or third hand? What parts appear to be guesswork and opinion?
4 Does the document contain information that can be corroborated in other sources? Does it contain any unique information?
5 Do the contents fit current historical opinion; or do they amplify or modify that opinion?
6 How far can the contents be assessed in terms of truth, ambiguity, omission, distortion and falsehood? (In a single document, one or all of these qualities can appear.)

D. Dymond (1981), *Writing Local History: A Practical Guide*, pp. 22–3.

Questions

1. Why does the author maintain that documents do not contain 'straightforward reproducible "truth" ' (lines 1–2)?
2. What questions would you pose about the structure and content of contemporary documents that you intend to use in social research?
3. How would you evaluate the strengths and weaknesses of documentary evidence?

☐ Evaluating Documentary Research

Sociologists need to evaluate continually the evidence that they use in their research. In evaluating documentary evidence questions need to be raised about authenticity, distortion and deception, availability and sampling and also presentation. It is issues such as these that are examined by Jennifer Platt.

Reading 3

Authenticity, in the sense where the alternative is forgery or mistaken authorship, can only apply to documents; as soon, however, as the sense is slightly broadened to cover other forms of incorrect identification or deliberate misrepresentation or use of false fronts, the essential problems are clearly the same as when the data are observations or reports of other kinds. The questions of existence and availability of desired documents have much in common with practical issues of access, perspective and social visibility in observational research. The status of different types of account and their recurring patterns, and how to evaluate it, is a quite general problem; the documentary researcher merely does not have the opportunity of the fieldworker to generate fresh data of the same or other kinds to get behind the original accounts, unless those who produced the documents are still alive. The problems of lack of choice in sampling and the need to construct one's own sampling frame, arise in many other types of research (even if they are not always confronted); documents have less propensity to move house or fail to co-operate than people, so may make the task easier. Methods of search for individuals in an unknown population of documents and of deciding when to stop searching, seem closely analogous to issues raised by 'snowball' samples for interviewing. The making of inferences from documents is in essence much like the making of inferences from other forms of behaviour, with the practical limitation again that there is likely to be less possibility of laying hands on supplementary information desirable to assist inference.

We conclude, therefore, that there are important senses in which documentary research has problems which are not significantly different from those of research using other data sources. A more general moral might be suggested, which is that the distinctions commonly made among 'methods' of research in terms of their data sources may be analytically unhelpful.

J. Platt (1981), 'Evidence and Proof in Documentary Research I', *Sociological Review*, Vol. 29, No. 1, p. 489.

Questions

1. Evaluate the advantages and disadvantages involved in doing documentary research and observational research.
2. Is sampling easier in documentary research? Give reasons for your answer.
3. Jennifer Platt states 'there are important senses in which documentary research has problems which are not significantly different from those of research using other data sources' (lines 26–28). Do you agree? If so why? If not, why not?

☐ The Oral Tradition

There are certain subjects that sociologists study where oral testimony becomes important. Every society has topics that are not discussed in written documents but which are transmitted orally. Oral history can provide material on such subjects and can help to counteract the bias of written records. Paul Thompson highlights some of the achievements of oral history in relation to his own work.

Reading 4

The Edwardians: the Remaking of British Society was originally conceived as an overall reassessment of the social history of the period, rather than a field-work venture. But I fairly soon discovered that although there was a wealth of printed publications from the early twentieth century, including numerous government papers and some pioneering sociological studies, much of what I wished to know was either treated from a single, unsatisfactory perspective, or altogether ignored. Manuscript material could not fill these gaps, because where normally accessible it simply enlarged on the bureaucratic perspectives already available in the printed sources. It was too recent a period for a satisfactory range of more personal documents to have reached the county record offices. I wanted to know what it was like to be a child or a parent at that time; how young people met and courted; how they lived together as husbands and wives; how they found jobs, moved between them; how they felt about work; how they saw their employers and fellow-workers; how they survived and felt when out of work; how class-consciousness varied between city, country and occupations. None of these questions seemed answerable from conventional historical sources, but when Thea Vigne and I began to collect the evidence of, eventually, some 500 interviews, the richness of information available through this method was at once apparent. Indeed, much more was collected than could be exploited in a single book, so that in the end *The Edwardians* became as much a beginning as a conclusion, and the interviews collected for it are already providing the basis for other historical studies. Nevertheless it does indicate something of the overall scope of oral sources for social history. Interviews provided a pervasive background to the book's interpretations; they were cited in all but two of twenty-two chapters; and some sections, particularly on the family, rely heavily on direct quotations. Equally important, as an antidote to the simplifications of an overall outline of social structure I was able to present fourteen accounts of real Edwardian families, drawn from a range of classes and places over Britain, but obstinately individual – 'the untidy reality upon which . . . both theoretical sociology and historical myth rest'.

P. Thompson (1978), *The Voice of the Past*, 2nd edition, pp. 86–7.

Questions

1. On what basis did Paul Thompson decide to use oral historical evidence?
2. How did Paul Thompson use oral evidence?
3. Outline and discuss how you would conduct an oral historical study of life in Britain in the 1950s and 1960s.

☐ Doing Life Histories

Researchers who wish to conduct 'life history' research have to gain access to informants and provide a rationale for their projects. Such accounts will include a discussion of the design, conduct and dissemination of the study. In his research for *The Professional Fence*, Carl Klockars covered these issues in a letter to his informant.

Reading 5

30 December 1971

Dear Mr Swoggi:
    We have never met. Since I know something about you I ought to tell you something about me. I'm first of all a professor of sociol-

ogy and criminology at Beaver College. I teach criminology, theory, research, etc. I've published some articles and for the past two years I have been writing and researching a major book. The topic of the book is the professional receiver of stolen goods. It can and will be an important and interesting book.

I have read everything ever written about the "fence." Most of it is junk. Fencing is an old occupation. The first time the word fence was used in print was 1610. Since then there have been some very famous fences both real and fictional. I wouldn't suppose you had ever heard of Jonathan Wild, Moll Cutpurse, or Isaac Solomons, but they were all major fences in the 18th and 19th centuries in England. Many real fences throughout history have been men with amazing abilities and almost giant characters. Such men, though, are few and far between.

There is surely an art to being a fence and there are but a very few great artists left. I have some suspicion that the art and character of fencing is dying or changing. There are certainly a lot of nickel-and-dime hustlers and pushers who will pick up swag for peanuts but they are not true professionals or artists of the caliber that the occupation of fencing has known.

During the past two years I have talked with close to a hundred thieves. The majority of them have been at the state prison. To date I have almost 50 hours of tape recorded interviews, stories, and anecdotes about fences and fencing.

I am not a cop. I can keep things confidential and there are quite a few guys who can give me "references." (Tommy Blue was the man who suggested that I write to you before I try to see you. Eyeball sends his regards.) Eyeball didn't give me any information that might be harmful to you. For one thing, I'm not interested in anything of that sort anyway.

Let me try to tell you what I am trying to write about. First, I want to try to describe the style and quality of the professional fence. How does he live? What does he do? Who are his friends? What kinds of people does he deal with? How does he handle them? Second, what kind of man must a fence be? Actor, businessman, artist, or hustler? What skills must he have? Why does he choose and stick with his business? Third, I'd like to know how the business has changed, both in the past ten or twenty years and since it began in the seventeenth century. Is amateur competition greater today than ten years ago? Is the old time fence a thing of the past? Do unprofessional thieves make for unprofessional fences? And fourth, I'd like to write about the fence as a "criminal without victims," a man whom thieves, the neighborhood, and his customers are glad to have around, a man with no direct victims.

I am not interested in any details which could get anyone in trouble. Names, dates, specific crimes, specific places, specific people are of no interest to me. If I were a cop, I'd have to warn you of your rights before talking to me. Since I tell you that I am not a cop and will not make any such warning, nothing that you say to me could be used against you. Also, as you are aware, there is a statute of limitations on receiving. It would be just as helpful to talk about things the way they were three years ago as they are today.

To be honest with you I'd like to write your biography. It could become a classic book. I'll call you during the first week of January. Please don't turn me down without letting me take you to lunch and tell you more.

Sincerely yours,

[*Signed*]

Carl Klockars

C. Klockars (1974), *The Professional Fence*, pp. 214–6.

Questions

1. From this letter, what do you understand to be the concern of 'life history' studies?
2. How does Klockars handle ethical issues?
3. Write a brief letter to another student requesting permission to do a 'life history' study of him or her, indicating the materials that you would like for the study.

☐ Understanding Texts

This chapter has examined a range of written and oral documentary sources. In addition, researchers can also use visual materials in their work. It is this range of documentary evidence that June Purvis refers to as 'texts'. Studies might draw on official documents, published commentaries, newspaper articles and personal material such as letters, diaries and photographs. But how might the researcher analyse and attempt to understand these texts? June Purvis suggests some possibilities and problems.

Reading 6

Descriptive analysis and perspective analysis
To sum up, then, we can treat the creators of texts as witnesses, and use their descriptions of the world to provide information

about events, people and places in which we are interested. Or we can treat them as representative of particular social groupings and use their texts for what they tell us about the perspectives of such groups. As a way of remembering these two uses to which texts can be put, we might call the first *descriptive analysis* and the second *perspective analysis.* Though these two types of analysis are analytically distinct, in practice historians and sociologists often blur the distinction between the two. Nevertheless, it is important to bear this distinction in mind when reading research based on the analysis of texts. This is because the checks that need to be made about the texts vary according to which kind of analysis is involved. With descriptive analysis, the accuracy of the account is the central concern, and in order to assess this, it is necessary to compare the accounts with others describing the same phenomenon. In the case of perspective analysis, however, the accuracy of the account does not necessarily matter. What is important is whether it is representative of the perspectives of the social category to which one is assigning the author(s) of the text. Once again, the text will be compared with others, but this time with those produced by other members of that social category.

The two types of analysis are complementary. In particular, perspective analysis may suggest ways in which the description of events in a text may be biased. For example, if we know that the author is a member of a political party, we will evaluate the information given in the light of that author's political perspective. Donald Mackinnon evaluates a speech delivered by Anthony Crosland at the North of England Education Conference on 7 January 1966. When Crosland delivered that speech, he was Secretary of State for Education in a Labour Government and a strong advocate of comprehensive schooling. In that speech, you may remember, Crosland said that the tripartite or bipartite system of schools that was established after the 1944 Education Act was 'educationally and socially unjust, inefficient, wasteful and divisive'.

Crosland was expressing social and political values, and he had definite views of what was 'good or bad, right or wrong, what should or should not be done'. Although Crosland does provide some evidence to support some of his claims, this evidence is referred to briefly and casually, not in a scholarly manner.

J. Purvis (1984), *Understanding Texts*, p. 10.

Questions

1. What do you understand by 'descriptive analysis' and 'perspective analysis'?
2. Why does June Purvis suggest 'the two types of analysis are complementary' (line 19)? Do you agree with her views?

3. Collect either the diary of an actor or actress or a speech by a Member of Parliament or an eye witness account of a strike. How would you evaluate the material you have chosen?

Project Questions

1. Consider the kinds of historical documents that could be used in a sociological study of your school or college.
2. What theoretical and practical issues need to be considered in preparing to conduct a series of oral history interviews?
3. What methodological issues are involved in using photographs in a sociological study? Consider this question in relation to photographs on a topic of your choice.

Further Reading

H. Becker, 'Introduction' (to the Jack Roller) in C. Shaw, *The Jack Roller* (University of Chicago Press, 1966; Phoenix edition), provides a classic statement on the advantages of using 'life history' data.

E.H. Carr, *What is History?* (Penguin, 1964), is a discussion of the basic issues concerning the relationship between history and sociology.

K. Plummer, *Documents of Life* (Allen and Unwin, 1983), is an excellent guide to life histories and other historical documents that examine situations from the participants' point of view.

J. Purvis, *Understanding Texts*, Open University Course E205, Unit 15 (Open University Press, 1984), provides a very good introduction to the problems involved in using texts in historical and sociological studies, together with a discussion of how researchers may attempt to solve them.

J. Scott, *A Matter of Record* (Polity Press, 1990), is a very good guide to methodological issues in documentary research.

P. Thompson, *The Voice of the Past: Oral History* (Oxford University Press, 1978), is a clear guide to the practicalities of conducting oral historical studies.

There are numerous studies that utilise documentary evidence. For further guides and examples, see Burgess (1982; 1984; 1985). The following collection has been selected for mention because it is based entirely on documentary research:

M. Bulmer (ed), *Mining and Social Change* (Croom Helm, 1978), is a collection of essays of life in North East England. See especially the personal accounts based on personal documents in Part 2.

8 | Mixing methods of social research

Many discussions of research methods focus on competing ideas. Debates occur about the relative merits of quantitative as opposed to qualitative methods, surveys as against participant observation and different theoretical positions that lead to the use of different methods. While these issues can be simply formulated into opposing points of debate among methodologists, they are not so easily handled in actual projects. Here, researchers need to begin with their research question before considering the methods of investigation that are to be used, for in practice it is essential to adopt a flexible approach by using those methods that are appropriate for the research questions that are posed. Accordingly, many researchers are involved in using a multi-method approach to their investigations.

The strategy of combining approaches to investigation is known by a variety of terms:

Combined operations is a term coined by Margaret Stacey that focuses on methods of investigation.

Mixed strategies is very similar, having been used by Jack Douglas to talk about the use of different research methods.

Triangulation is the most frequently used term, which has been identified by Norman Denzin to highlight the use of different methods, investigators, data and theories within a study.

Multiple strategies is a term that I have found useful to discuss the way in which different methods, data, investigators and theories may be used to overcome bias within a study. In addition, it also allows for the integration of approaches within a project.

The four main strategies used by researchers are:

Multiple methods that may involve the use of different research techniques in relation to the same topic of study or the same method on different occasions.

Multiple investigators refers to studies being conducted by teams rather than by individuals. Teams may be used to bring together researchers from different disciplinary backgrounds or with different kinds of personal experience or to bring to a study differences in terms of gender, ethnicity, age and social class.

Multiple data sets may be obtained through the use of different methods, or also as a consequence of using the same method at different times or with different sources.

Multiple theories is closely linked with multiple sets of data and the analysis of the data. At an initial stage of analysis, different theories and hypotheses may be tried out in relation to the research data or competing hypotheses may be examined.

By using different approaches to social investigation, a researcher may obtain different sets of data. Indeed, the differences may help the researcher much more in understanding a social situation than when similar data are obtained. A key point of debate is between those who consider that data can be integrated, as opposed to those who favour complementarity. While links are often made between theory and method which suggests a direct correspondence between surveys and positivist epistemology and between qualitative methods and interpretative epistemology, it is seldom as straightforward. Indeed, the choice of methods may not be made purely on theoretical grounds. Nevertheless, a case can be made for combining methods of investigation in order to examine different levels of a social situation and to focus on different aspects of the same problem. Overall, the use of multiple strategies may result in a precise statement of the aims of using each method, the data that are obtained and the way those data relate to theory. Obviously, by working in this way researchers will find contradictions that need to be explored within the project.

The use of multiple strategies in social research is also influenced by a range of other considerations including the funding context, the availability and organisation of a research team and the value position of the investigator. Some sponsors may specify the kind of approach that is to be adopted or the data sets that are required. This in turn will lead to specifying not only the kinds of methods that are required, but also the skills demanded of researchers who constitute the research team. Finally, the values of research team members may suggest one approach rather than another. Indeed, some feminists such as Ann Oakley and Hilary Graham have argued against the use of surveys and in favour of qualitative approaches, as the latter methods render women more visible. Meanwhile, Liz Stanley and Sue Wise suggest that feminist research may involve using and combining a rich range of methods. Certainly, recent discussions of multiple strategies of investigation suggest that: quantitative work can complement and facilitate qualitative work; qualitative work can complement and facilitate quantitative work; both approaches can be used with equal emphasis. Overall, much will depend upon the research and the researcher and will continue to be the subject of discussion and debate among those who conduct social research.

☐ A Case for Mixing Methods

Social scientists need to consider the advantages and disadvantages of methods of social investigation in relation to their research problems. In this reading, Martin Trow puts the case for working with a range of methodological tools.

Reading 1

Every cobbler thinks leather is the only thing. Most social scientists, including the present writer, have their favorite methods with which they are familiar and have some skill in using. And I suspect we mostly choose to investigate problems that seem vulnerable to attack through these methods. But we should at least try to be less parochial than cobblers. Let us be done with the arguments of "participant observation" *versus* interviewing – as we have largely dispensed with the arguments for psychology *versus* sociology – and get on with the business of attacking our problems with the widest array of conceptual and methodological tools that we possess and they demand. This does not preclude discussion and debate regarding the relative usefulness of different methods for the study of specific problems or types of problems. But that is very different from the assertion of the general and inherent superiority of one method over another on the basis of some intrinsic qualities it presumably possesses.

M. Trow (1957), 'Comment on Participant Observation and Interviewing: a comparison', *Human Organisation*, Vol. 16, p. 35.

Questions

1. What are the methodological problems of a researcher having favourite methods?
2. Are debates about participant observation versus interviewing redundant? If so, why? If not, why not?

3. What is the relative usefulness of participant observation and interviews in studies of:
   (a) children's use of television
   (b) members of a religious sect
   (c) football hooligans?

☐ Triangulation

Of all the terms used to describe the way in which a combination of methods can be used in social research, Norman Denzin's term 'triangulation' is most commonly used. However, as Denzin indicates in this reading, this approach can be applied to a range of research strategies.

Reading 2

Triangulation, or the use of multiple methods, is a plan of action that will raise sociologists above the personalistic biases that stem from single methodologies. By combining methods and investigators in the same study, observers can partially overcome the deficiencies that flow from one investigator and/or one method. Sociology as a science is based on the observations generated from its theories, but until sociologists treat the act of generating observations as an act of symbolic interaction, the links between observations and theories will remain incomplete. In this respect triangulation of method, investigator, theory, and data remains the soundest strategy of theory construction.

It is conventionally assumed that triangulation is the use of multiple methods in the study of the same object (see Campbell and Fiske, 1959; Webb, *et al.*, 1966). Indeed, this is the generic definition I have offered, but it is only one form of the strategy. It is convenient to conceive of triangulation as involving varieties of data, investigators, and theories, as well as methodologies. The four basic types of triangulation are *data*, with these types; (1) time, (2) space, (3) person, and these levels (1) aggregate (person), (2) interactive (person), (3) collectivity (person); *investigator* (multiple vs. single observers of same object); *theory* (multiple vs. single perpectives in relation to the same set of objects); and *methodological* (within-method triangulation and between method triangulation).

N. Denzin (1970), *The Research Act*, pp. 300–1.

Questions

1. What do you understand by the term 'triangulation'?

2. Is triangulation 'the soundest strategy of theory construction'? Give reasons for your answer.
3. Norman Denzin outlines different types of data triangulation. Explain how these types of data triangulation could be used in a study of your school or college.

☐ Combining Quantitative and Qualitative Research

Several researchers have highlighted distinctions between quantitative and qualitative research rather than focusing on ways in which they can complement each other. In this reading, Alan Bryman discusses the way in which Herbert Gans combined methods in his study of Levittown.

Reading 3

One of the contexts in which quantitative and qualitative research are most frequently united is where an ethnographer carries out a survey in order to fill some gaps in his or her knowledge of a community, group, organization, or whatever, because the gaps cannot be readily filled by a reliance on participant observation or unstructured interviewing alone. Such gaps may occur for a variety of reasons, such as the inaccessibility either of particular people or of particular situations.

In his study of a new suburban community in the USA (known as Levittown, after the name of the builders), Gans (1967) made much greater use of questionnaires and formal interviewing (although participant observation was the dominant method) than in his earlier ethnographic research on a working class area in Boston (Gans, 1962). Gans was interested in the ways in which a new community comes about and in the nature and effects of suburban life. Consequently, a major component of his proposed investigation entailed attention to people's aspirations, expectations and reasons for moving prior to their departure from the city to suburbia. In addition, a follow-up was required to examine changes in orientations after moving into suburbia and the consequences of suburban living for the individual. These are highly specific questions which required access to people prior to their arrival and systematic information on changes in their views over time. Gans used a postal questionnaire which was sent to 3,100 individuals who were on the point of moving to Levittown. The data deriving from this exercise provided Gans with information about respondents' reasons for moving. In addition, structured interviews were carried out with a small sample of Levittowners to find out about their hopes and expectations before moving in, and again two years later to determine the changes that had occurred for them. This information provided data on feelings of loneliness and boredom and also allowed Gans to establish changes in attitudes and behaviour over the two-year period. Interestingly, Gans did not himself conduct these interviews (which were carried out by graduate students) because he felt that his participant observation cast him in the role of resident, so that he could less readily ask personal questions. These quantitative data were combined with Gans's participant observation in the community to provide a rounded portrayal of people's experiences of suburban living.

A. Bryman (1988), *Quantity and Quality in Social Research*, pp. 137–8.

Questions

1. Why did Gans use a questionnaire and formal interviews in his study?
2. In what way were structured interviews used in Gans' study?
3. Do you agree with Gans' reasons for not conducting the interviews personally? Give reasons for your answer.

☐ Some Problems of Integrating Methods

While there have been some strong advocates for methodological integration, it is important for researchers to reflect on the ways in which studies successfully integrate methods and the barriers to their use. In this reading we examine issues of integration.

Reading 4

I should note some of the reasons why the systematic merging of data sources in a single study has been rare. There is no shortage of cases in which a second method has been used as a supplement to a primary source of data, as when anthropologists use surveys as an adjunct to field observation, or survey researchers use observation as a prelude to questionnaire construction. But the number of studies in which different methods have entered the research design more or less as equals has been small, and those in which the intersections of these methods have been discussed in detail are even fewer. The following seem to be the main obstacles to methodological integration in social research.

Limited competence

Probably the greatest single barrier to methodological integration is the sheer lack of capacity to draw on methods other than the one in which one was originally trained. It is both a strength and a weakness of professional training in the social sciences that aspirants to the various disciplines typically learn but one major approach to data collection. It is a strength because competence in one method provides the foundation for high-quality research and works against the shallowness of multidisciplinary omniscence. Donald Campbell has warned about the dangers of creating social scientists who are competent in everything but proficient at nothing. But the narrowness of methodological training becomes intellectually counterproductive when the skills acquired blind social scientists to the complementary potential of other approaches. For the future the best route towards greater integration may not be training in two or three different approaches, for that strategy runs the risk of superficiality, but rather teaching these professionals to understand and appreciate the contribution of other data sources. Interestingly, in his research on Peruvian communities Whyte, whose methodological forte was participant observation, did not try to become an instant expert on survey research. Instead he entered into collaboration with a colleague whose own strong suit was survey research, and through joint work over a period of years came to understand and use that methodology.

Disciplinary ethnocentrism

A second and closely related barrier to integration is the tendency of the various social science disciplines or subdisciplines to exalt the virtues of their dominant methods and disparage those of other fields. Thus many quantitative social scientists fancy themselves as 'hard-heads' – true scientists whose propensity for numbers betokens a deep and undying commitment to truth. Those who do not share this faith are 'soft heads' who do not deserve the name of science. For their part social scientists of a qualitative persuasion often portray their approach as humane, sensitive, intuitive, and comprehensive. In this world view the participant observer is a caring, pulsating human being who identifies with the people being studied and learns as much by being as by doing. Quantitative researchers, by contrast, are methodologically gross, insensitive to contexts and more often than not wrong in their assessment of community dynamics. Happily these stereotypical images of social research are less common than in earlier decades, but they are by no means dead. Their practical consequence is that they make self-respecting social scientists from one tradition at least initially wary of associating too closely with those of a different persuasion.

Costs

Even for those who would like to take up some form of integration, the costs, financial and otherwise, are often high. Projects drawing together two or three different data sources are not only more expensive than those relying on one method, but much more complicated to carry out. What economists call 'transactions costs' are exceptionally high in interdisciplinary projects. At the beginning specialists from the different disciplines, whatever their commitment to the overarching objectives of the project, may have difficulty communicating with each other about methodology. The survey specialist may wonder why anthropological research takes so long, and the anthropologist may question how survey research can ever hope to gather valid data through such brief contacts with respondents. If the aim of the project is to bring about an integration of data sources from the outset, lengthy discussion may be needed to work out a suitable fit among the approaches used. If, on the other hand, each specialist goes his or her way at the beginning, the problem of integration will simply be postponed until later. In short, anyone who thinks that methodological integration is an easy task – financially, psychologically, intellectually, or administratively – has obviously never tried it. But the benefits particularly the possibility of checking key areas of information by earlier independent sources, make these costs worth bearing.

Opportunities

Finally, a major barrier to methodological integration is the lack of suitable projects for combining methods. Partly this is a matter of financing, for funding agencies often resist studies that appear complex and cost more than those with simpler methodologies. But also at work in many countries is a second-order effect of professional training. Planners with a background in economics may see no need for studies drawing on anthropological methods, particularly when the village research involved requires 1 or 2 years of work in just a few areas. Even if the researchers were to explain the enormous advantages of that fieldwork for policy purposes, the administrators will often ask why the same task cannot be accomplished with more rapid and preferably quantitative methods. Similarly, the problems of integration faced by the researchers themselves, such as how qualitative and quantitative research on villages can best be brought together, will also be problems for sponsors and administrators who have to approve such efforts. Given the paucity of successful cases of methodological integration, there is hardly a book that proponents can bring forth as an illustration of what is to come. There is a vicious circle here in which the absence of live examples of integration makes it difficult to convince funders and other key decision-makers about the feasibility and benefits of multiple data sources.

D.P. Warwick (1983), 'On Methodological Integration in Social Research' in M. Bulmer and D.P. Warwick (eds), *Social Research in Developing Countries*, pp. 293–5.

Questions

1. Do you think social scientists should be trained in a range of different methods? Give reasons for your answer.
2. Do you think the costs of methodological integration are worth bearing? Give reasons for your answer.
3. Choose any study with which you are familiar and evaluate it in terms of its use of methodological integration.

☐ Combining Methods: An Example

The scale of the research problem defined in some studies demands a range of research methods for effective data collection. In this reading, Penelope Weston and her colleagues discuss the methods used in a study of whole curriculum management across the 5–16 age range since the 1988 Education Reform Act.

Reading 5

The initial research design started from two assumptions:

- that in order to review the development of whole curriculum management in response to ERA it would be necessary to confine the study to a small number of schools;

- that the 5–16 span of the National Curriculum called for linked studies of primary and secondary schools.

We also wished to take account of the LEA curriculum policy and support; and to consider how to put case-study findings into a national context.

The three LEA case studies

The LEAs

The three LEAs were invited to participate as a result of a selection process to identify LEAs representing varying geographic and socio-economic areas. All three were thought to have strong curriculum policies and had undertaken, or were embarking on, major curriculum development initiatives with their schools. Although one LEA had some middle schools, it was decided to confine the case studies to primary and secondary schools and to limit the enquiry to the 5–16 age range. The three LEAs all agreed to participate. For the report they have each been given a pseudonym: Metroland (the outer London Borough), Midshire (the Midlands county) and Norweston (the north-western urban LEA).

Selecting the schools

Each of the three LEAs was asked to identify one or more 'families' of schools who might be invited to participate. The process of approaching schools varied in each case. Only one LEA (Midshire) had a formal 'family' structure for its schools. In the event, only some of the schools in the family which was suggested for the study were able to participate fully. Schools from two other nearby families were also visited, therefore, to balance the evidence from the main family. In Norweston, the secondary school (St Luke's) was suggested by the LEA and a number of feeder primary schools in the same town were then visited. As a church school, St Luke's drew pupils from a large number of schools, but the main feeder schools were within the same town. In all, three were invited and agreed to take part, representing different traditions and settings within the local area. One primary was actually in an adjacent LEA, but many of its pupils went on to St Luke's. In Metroland the situation was more complex because there were no natural catchment areas; indeed, secondary pupils travelled extensively within and across LEA boundaries. A number of secondary schools were visited, and it was eventually decided to invite two secondary schools to take part. Four primary schools which sent pupils to one or both of these secondaries also agreed to participate.

Working with the schools

The schools were all visited a number of times during 1990, from the spring term through until the autumn. The school case studies had two main phases. In the first, the main aim was to obtain a full account of the school's curriculum policy, by interviewing a wide range of staff, including all senior managers, many middle managers (heads of department and year, teachers with responsibility for special needs, INSET, assessment and other whole-school briefs), and some classroom teachers. In addition, curriculum planning and organisation documents were collected and reviewed. Contacts were also maintained with LEA staff, particularly those in the advisory service or inspectorate with responsibility for the case-study schools. As a result of this first phase, certain priorities were identified for further investigation in specific schools. In addition to pursuing the 'story' of whole curriculum management in each school, as it unfolded from the school year 1989/90 into 1990/91, the other priorities included special needs, assessment, flexible learning, cross-phase collaboration and INSET. These issues were followed up in later visits to the schools, which included further interviews, attendance at planning meetings, some classroom observation and participation in INSET events. Finally, governors at each case-study school were invited to respond to a short questionnaire on their involvement in curriculum policy and management. This was sent out by the schools to chairs of governors and to parent and community governors. All but two of the 16 schools provided a reponse, but the overall total was low: 36 questionnaires were returned.

Other inquiries
During the period of the study, the researchers participated in other events and visits within the three LEAs, including visits to other schools, LEA INSET events and interviews with LEA staff. In the spring of 1990, an exploratory survey was undertaken in non-case-study schools, to identify curriculum management priorities and to check whether the issues emerging in the case-study schools were typical of concerns in the LEA as a whole. Each LEA was asked to suggest schools for this small-scale survey and the size and nature of the sample varied. In all, 46 primaries and 13 secondaries responded. The responses indicated that the case-study schools were fairly typical in their concerns. Central to these was the sheer volume and range of curriculum priorities that had to be managed. At that stage, for example, a number of issues, including assessment, were being deferred in many schools until the national requirements were clarified; but worry about special needs support and problems in managing cross-curricular elements were already being identified in both primary and secondary schools. In reporting on this small survey, it was noted that there had been no question in it about cross-phase curriculum continuity, which was already emerging as a key issue in the case-study 'families'.

Regional groups
One other strategy for widening the context of the case studies
was the creation of review groups centred on each of the LEAs.
Representatives from up to five neighbouring LEAs were invited to
meet in their case-study LEA to discuss some aspect of the
research, and compare developments and approaches in their
own areas. Three such meetings were held in each of the three
LEAs during 1990. These meetings proved a very useful element of
the study, providing a forum for frank discussion of differing
approaches to issues such as cross-phase continuity, curriculum
coverage, LEA support for and monitoring of schools and assessment policies. In addition, a number of the LEA representatives
agreed to be interviewed in depth about LEA organisation, whole-
curriculum policies and schools' response to ERA.

The national survey
The national survey was scheduled for the final stage of the project, in order to review, on this wider scale, the issues which had
proved most significant within the case studies. A sample of 1,400
maintained primary, middle and secondary schools was drawn,
stratified by region and LEA type (metropolitan and other LEAs).
Some smaller schools (primaries with fewer than 60 pupils, secondaries with fewer than 120) were specifically included in the sample. Two versions of the questionnaire were developed, one for
primary and middle schools and one for secondary schools,
although there were a number of common questions. A draft version was trialled with schools in several LEAs and the final revised
version was sent to schools in the autumn term of 1990. The
questionnaire focussed on whole-curriculum management and had
five sections:

   1 Staffing and development
   2 Planning the whole curriculum
   3 Implementing the whole curriculum
   4 School details
   5 Reviewing whole-curriculum strategies.

P. Weston and E. Barrett with J. Jamison (1992), *The Quest for Coherence*,
pp. 217–19.

Questions

1. How did the research problem on managing the whole curriculum suggest a combination of research methods?
2. Explain the role of
   (a) case studies
   (b) the national survey
in this study.

3. Are the case studies and the national survey integrated or complementary in this project? Give reasons for your answer.

☐ Using Restudies and Team Research

Among the strategies that researchers have used to engage in triangulation is the restudy of an institution or locality and the use of research teams. In this reading, William Foote Whyte discusses these approaches.

Reading 6

In the Chancay Valley, with Huayopampa and Pacaraos, we had teams of two to six people in the community at the same time. The results showed the value of team efforts. A team can provide for a division of labor, with one individual examining the records of the communal government, observing *junta* meetings, and interviewing about local government activities, and another concentrating on the organization of economic activities and the measurement of income. A team also provides protection against the biases of a single individual. In the course of the field period, the team members learn from each other as they spend hours discussing and comparing their findings and arguing about interpretations.

We had originally hoped that during 1964 we would complete not only the surveys but also the anthropological studies in each of our villages. Between 1964 and 1969 we had planned only brief field expeditions to check anything that might have changed since the previous studies. Instead of simply bringing each village up to date, we carried out full-scale restudies to check the original findings, fill in gaps and reexamine interpretations made on the basis of the original study.

In some cases, restudies revealed serious errors in the previous work. Our first study of one community described an unusual type of committee functioning under the local government. The restudy provided no information on this committee. When we checked with the research team of the restudy, we found that the committee in question did not exist and had never existed. How could such a mistake be made? The student who did the first study described the committee on the basis of information given him by a single informant. This informant had a record for urging changes that frequently were not carried out. The minutes of the meetings of local government record the establishment of the committee, but the idea was never implemented.

In another community, after making a much more careful and systematic examination of the economic aspects of community life, our restudy team developed figures indicating that the first study's family income estimate was twice as large as it should have been. It might be argued that such errors can be avoided by a good anthropologist using good methods. I agree that a well-trained and experienced anthropologist will bring in more adequate field data than will beginning students, but the history of social anthropology should raise doubts about the wisdom of relying entirely upon the field reports of a single anthropologist, no matter how well trained or how large his or her professional reputation.

The checking and rechecking process also stimulated our students to raise their standards of performance. They explained to us, "The information you had was simply wrong because the man who made the study got it from a single informant and did not check it with anybody else." Or, "Those original income estimates were just based on sloppy methods. We have talked with X, and he has admitted that this part of his study was not good." The students were thinking not only of professors who would read their reports, but also of future students who would follow them and check on their work.

The quality of our studies has been improved by the writing of comparative descriptions and analyses about pairs or sets of communities. When a research director reads reports on communities, A and B, deficiencies may escape his attention until he is required to write a comparison of the two. He then finds that he has excellent information on one aspect of life in community A, but the information from community B does not refer to some points considered important by the writers of the A report. For example, impressed by the Pacaraos report on the low frequency of collection of fines, we looked for comparable data in the Huayopampa monograph – and did not find any. Since Huayopampans paid 100 percent of their fines, collection did not seem a problem and was not reported. When we compared the two villages, Huayopampa's success in collecting fines was clearly as important as Pacaraos's failure.

W.F. Whyte (1984), *Learning From The Field*, pp. 139–40.

Questions

1. What are the merits and demerits of team research?
2. Assess the value of restudies in social research.
3. What is the value of comparative descriptions and analyses in research projects?

Project Questions

1. Outline and design a study which uses both survey methods and ethnographic methods. What advantages and disadvantages are involved in using these styles of investigation?
2. Consider the way in which a research team could be used to conduct a small-scale project in your school or college. Assess the strengths and weaknesses of a team-based approach.
3. How can different methods be used to cross-check data sets in a research project of your choice?

Further Reading

J. Brannen (ed), *Mixing Methods: Qualitative and Quantitative Research* (Avebury, 1992), provides a set of papers on the quantitative vs qualitative debate, together with examples.

A. Bryman, *Quantity and Quality in Social Research* (Unwin Hyman, 1988; republished by Routledge), provides a detailed outline of the debate in this area.

M. Bulmer (ed), *Sociological Research Methods* (Macmillan, 1977), focuses on the link between theory and method.

R.G. Burgess (ed), *Field Research: A Sourcebook and Field Manual* (Allen and Unwin, 1982; republished by Routledge), includes a set of papers on combining methods of investigation.

R.G. Burgess, *In The Field: An Introduction to Field Research* (Allen and Unwin, 1984; republished by Routledge), includes a chapter on multiple strategies.

Empirical Studies

All the studies recommended throughout this volume can be examined for their use of multiple strategies. In particular, see for example:

P. Carlen, D. Gleeson and J. Wardlaugh, *Truancy: The Politics of Compulsory Schooling* (Open University Press, 1992).

H.J. Gans, *The Urban Villagers* (Free Press, 1962).

M. Stacey, E. Batstone, C. Bell and A. Murcott, *Power, Persistence and Change* (Routledge and Kegan Paul, 1975).

9 | Ethical issues in social research

All the approaches to research that have been examined in this volume present the researcher with a series of ethical problems concerned with choosing topics to investigate, designing a project, collecting data, analysing data and writing reports. In this respect, a key role for the researcher is to develop ways in which ethical problems can be handled while doing research.

Sociology and social research covers all areas of social life. Yet we need to consider whether all areas of social life can be the subject of social investigation. Researchers need to consider whether they will be granted access to the social situations they wish to investigate and the circumstances in which it is appropriate to conduct research. In considering these issues, it is not only important for researchers to assess the situation that is to be researched, but also to assess their own skills, experiences and expertise to conduct the investigation.

Often when researchers assess a situation they need to consider whether the methods that are to be used are ethically justifiable. For example, several sociological studies have achieved notoriety as sociologists have conducted covert studies (that is, studies which were unknown to the research participants), as opposed to overt studies where permission had been sought to conduct the investigation.

Within the research literature there is a major debate about the use of covert as opposed to overt research. Much of this debate deals with the conduct of research in extreme situations and is concerned with such issues as deception, misrepresentation and manipulation. Yet these issues can arise in day-to-day situations that are examined by social researchers. Accordingly, all researchers need to consider carefully the circumstances in which they conduct research. While choices are made to conduct overt rather than covert research, it is rare to find situations where projects occur that are either completely overt or completely covert. Many 'grey areas' exist in social investigations which result in studies that cannot be governed by a set of rules.

Nevertheless, social research is surrounded by legislation, codes of professional conduct and statements of ethical principles which have all been designed to protect members of the public in their dealings with social researchers. In the last decade, several countries have established data protection laws (e.g. the Data Protection Act 1984 in the UK) which deal with human rights, privacy, confidentiality, anonymity and control of data collection and data processing. These issues can have an effect on data handling, data analysis and the secondary analysis of existing data sets where restrictions are placed on the use and disclosure of data.

In response to such situations, many of the major professional associations have also established codes of ethics and statements of ethical principles which are designed to promote good practice among social scientists in their dealings with members of the public. For example, the British Sociological Association has a statement of ethical principles that deals with a range of topics including professional integrity, relations and responsibilities to research participants, covert research, anonymity and confidentiality, as well as relations and responsibilities to sponsors and funders, together with the implications for data dissemination.

Central to many of these discussions is the principle of informed consent. This principle is based upon four issues. First, that all those aspects of what might occur, or is to occur, are disclosed to those who agree to participate in the project. Secondly, that this information is communicated to the individual in a way that is easily understood. Thirdly, that the individual who is to be researched is capable of assessing the situation and making a mature judgement on it. Finally that there should be an agreement to participate in the project. While this may seem simple and reasonable, it is not easy to apply in practice. Some research projects are very complex and the researcher cannot always indicate what may occur during the course of the project. Furthermore, projects may be explained to individuals, but that is no guarantee that they can envisage what will transpire, especially if they have not participated in a research project before.

Such situations underline the fact that although governments, social scientists and sociologists have established frameworks in which research can be conducted, they cannot eliminate all the problems associated with social investigation. Accordingly, it is a key task for the investigator to examine carefully the ethical dilemmas that present themselves on a day-by-day basis when conducting research. It is by considering ethical issues in practice that we are able to find 'solutions' to difficult social situations and to engage in rigorous evaluation and self-evaluation of projects which allow us to understand the compromises made when using research methods and doing social research.

☐ Doing Covert Research

The key debate concerning the ethics of social research is whether research should be completely open (overt) or closed (covert). Much depends on the topic chosen. Several writers have objected to covert research on the grounds that it is deceptive. In this reading, Jason Ditton outlines a piece of covert ethnographic research he conducted in a bakery he called Wellbread's.

Reading 1

I decided to return to Wellbread's (where I had previously worked in undergraduate vacations) and concentrate upon whether or not workers paid by the hour exhibited logically similar actions to the patterns of 'output restriction' noticed amongst workers paid by the piece.

Although the graduate grant didn't start until October 1971, I worked through the summer of 1971 as a plant worker, *né* under-cover participant observer, at Wellbread's. By now, of course, I knew most of the men, and had none of the usual problems of getting permission, getting into the field, getting accepted, or get-ting going. In fact (and this, I suggest, is perhaps the mark of the truly accepted observer) I had far greater problems in getting *out*. My every attempt to leave, each timid suggestion that I might dis-cuss 'research plans', was brushed aside, and I was plied with furious pleas to stay and help the management out in the perennial summer labour shortage period!

Nevertheless, I *was* able to develop personal covert participant-observation skills. Right from the start, I found it impossible to keep everything that I wanted to remember in my head until the end of the working day (some of the shifts were over twelve hours long) and so had to take rough notes as I was going along. But I was stuck 'on the line', and had nowhere to retire to privately to jot things down. Eventually, the wheeze of using innocently provided lavatory cubicles occurred to me. Looking back, all my notes for that third summer were on Bronco toilet paper! Apart from the awkward tendency for pencilled notes to be self-erasing from hard toilet paper (sometimes before I could even get home), my fre-quent requests for 'time out' after interesting happenings or conversations in the bakehouse and the amount of time that I was spending in the lavatory began to get noticed. I had to pacify some genuinely concerned work-mates, give up totally undercover operations, and 'come out' as an observer – albeit in a limited way. I eventually began to scribble notes more openly, but still not in front of people when they were talking. When questioned about this, as I was occasionally, I coyly said that I was writing things down that occurred to me about 'my studies'.

J. Ditton (1977), *Part-Time Crime: An Ethnography of Fiddling and Pilferage*, pp. 4–5.

Questions

1. Was Jason Ditton justified in claiming that he had no access problems just because he had worked at Wellbread's before, or did his research position pose new problems? Give reasons for your answer.
2. Why do you think covert participant observation was used to study fiddling and pilferage? List the advantages and disadvantages of taking this role.
3. Jason Ditton discusses the ways he took notes for his studies in front of some workers. To what extent does this make his study semi-covert?

☐ Problems of Covert Participant Observation

Among the studies around which there has been considerable debate are those that use covert ethnographic methods. In this reading, Martin Bulmer examines the problems of covert participant observation in pseudo-patient studies where researchers pretend to be patients.

Reading 2

Pseudo-patient studies clearly demonstrate the limitations of the use of covert methods in sociological research. Though apparently providing good access to otherwise unobtainable data, the method is shown to be a difficult one to use, with consequences for research subjects, observer, other participants and for the credibility of sociology more generally. It is also of interest that Caudill and Redlich, like John Lofland, apparently reflected and repented over the years, concluding that the earlier use of covert methods was not justified. Is this an approach to research which callow youth are prone to employ, while the same people when older and wiser fight shy of it?

Dingwall is surely right to emphasise that trust is at the heart of the fieldwork relationship. 'In the last analysis, ethical fieldwork turns on the moral sense and integrity of the researcher negotiating the social contract which leads his subjects to expose their lives.' Stanton and Schwartz, for example, emphasise the benefits flowing from a relationship of confidence and trust with members of the hospital which they studied.

We do not believe that this real collaboration could possibly have arisen had we not followed our general principles fairly consistently. If the investigators had in fact been 'using' the personnel and patients as experimental objects or as instruments, a subtle but important reserve would have grown up inevitably; we suspect it would have concealed more than would have been learned from any freedom of action we would have gained.

The broader ethical issues of how the sociologist is regarded by others is also a relevant consideration, and connects with Sissela Bok's point about the corrupting influence of the widespread use of deception in social relationships.

We need to ask ourselves how much surveillance and infiltration we really want. Do we also want pseudo-patients in the classrooms, pseudo-converts to religious creeds, pseudo-party members, clients and patients? How far do we want to go to train some to spy on their fellows in order to find a few miscreants?

That this is not altogether remote from reality is suggested by jokes about Californian sects with four members, two of whom are sociologists doing covert research.

M. Bulmer (1982), 'The Research Ethics of Pseudo-Patient Studies', *Sociological Review*, Vol. 30, No. 4, pp. 641–2.

Questions

1. List the difficulties of using covert methods in pseudo-patient studies.
2. Examine the consequences of using covert methods in research for
   (a) the research subjects
   (b) the researcher
   (c) other participants
   (d) sociology more generally.
3. Is covert research spying? Discuss the case for and against using this approach in studies of
   (a) students
   (b) shoplifters
   (c) hospital patients.

☐ Ethical Issues in Survey Research

The literature on research ethics tends to confine the discussion very narrowly to ethical issues in participant observation and ethnography, yet some collections of essays (e.g. Burgess, 1989) indicate that it is an issue in all forms of research. In this reading, the authors consider ethical principles in relation to survey work.

Reading 3

Ethical principles in survey research, we suggest, concern the proper conduct of relationships between researchers and three groups of people: resource-providers, data subjects and a broad amorphous group that we shall call 'the public'. There is of course an overlap here: data subjects *are* key resource-providers in the research production process.

With respect to providers of resources, such as funders or employers, researchers should clarify their obligations in advance, and honour them honestly. As a general rule, resource-providers should not have rights of confidentiality; nor should any intellectual property rights allow them to inhibit publication of results. This latter is especially important for methodological aspects of the research, which should be explicated for dissemination and public appraisal. The prior existence of suitable codes of conduct can strengthen the researcher's hand in ensuring that these conditions are incorporated into any written contracts.

A particular group of resource-providers whose importance may be overlooked are the 'gatekeepers' who control access to sampling frames and/or sample members. Relationships between gatekeepers and researchers are often determined more by bargaining power and by the dictates of sound business practice than by any lofty ethical ideals. However, where the gatekeeper has a personal relationship with the data subject (for example, as proxy, parent, or teacher), researchers should be sensitive to the nature of that relationship and to the private spaces which it maintains. This does not necessarily mean that one should accept the gatekeeper's word as final, especially where the gatekeeper is in a position of considerable power over the data subjects.

With respect to data subjects, researchers should be conscious of their intrusive potential, and should seek to minimize any intrusion; the confidentiality of data must be respected and protected by positive measures; and data subjects should be told the purposes of the research and should have adequate opportunity to

withhold their co-operation. (This last is the principle of 'informed consent'.) 'Snooping' and 'voyeurism', and intrusive questioning which may merely reflect a hobby or passing interest on the part of the researcher, should be avoided (Huizer, 1973, p. 170).
With respect to the public, researchers should pursue openness, sensitivity, accuracy, honesty and objectivity in their choice of topic, methods, analysis and dissemination. This includes respecting the interests of different groups in society; avoiding research designs which preclude particular outcomes of the enquiry; disseminating findings fully, as well as widely; and facilitating the re-use of data.

D. Raffe, I. Blundell, and J. Bibby (1989), 'Ethics and Tactics: issues arising from an educational survey' in R.G. Burgess (ed), *The Ethics of Educational Research*, pp. 16–17.

Questions

1. List the issues you would want to clarify in advance of a survey with
   (a) a sponsor
   (b) a gatekeeper.
2. In what ways would you seek to minimise intrusion for data subjects?
3. What do you think researchers should do to maintain good relationships with the public?

☐ Principles of Data Protection

In recent years a considerable number of countries have passed legislation to protect personal data. These laws relate to human rights and personal privacy, freedom of information and security. A major concern is the abuse of data by governments. In this reading, Anne Akeroyd discusses some of the principles and purposes of data laws.

Reading 4

In most cases the law is administered or monitored by a data protection agency which may licence or register the holding, uses and, in some cases, the collection of personal data, their transfer abroad, and so on; it may have inspection and control functions, and be responsible for protecting the rights of data subjects. Breaches of the law may be sanctioned in some way, e.g. be punishable by fines, imprisonment, the forfeiture, erasure or destruction of data, or refusal of a licence, registration or concessions. In these matters there is considerable variation; most notably, there is no agency responsible for ensuring compliance with the U.S. Privacy Act.

The laws therefore provide for the protection of privacy, confidentiality and anonymity. In relation to data protection we can (briefly) say that:

- *Privacy* refers to the state of the person. The laws may specify what can be collected and held about whom and in what form. Particularly important in the privacy and data protection debate has been Westin's view (1967, p. 7) that privacy is a basic human need, and that: 'Privacy is the claim of individuals, groups or institutions to determine for themselves when, how and to what extent information about them is communicated to others'. In the wake of the data protection debate, Austria, Spain, Portugal, the Netherlands (and potentially, Switzerland) have upgraded protection for personal data to a fundamental human right by making constitutional provision for data protection (Hondius 1985, pp. 91–2);
- *Confidentiality* refers to the state of the data, the way they are handled, stored, protected, used and disseminated to third parties;
- *Anonymity* refers to the state of the identity. In data protection this involves issues about the holding of data in an identifiable or personalized form and whether or not a link can be made between an individual and a data item. Once the data are depersonalized the law has no further interest in them;
- *Data Protection* (*Datenschutz*) 'denotes the legal rules designed to assure the protection of individuals with regard to the storage, processing and dissemination of personal data relating to them, particularly where this is done with the aid of computers' (Hondius 1978, p. 61). Increasingly 'data protection' rather than 'privacy protection' is being used in relation to legislation, thereby allowing for the protection of data relating to legal persons as well as human ones.

A.V. Akeroyd (1988), 'Ethnography, Personal Data and Computers' in R.G. Burgess (ed), *Conducting Qualitative Research*, p. 183.

Questions

1. What criteria would you use to devise a Data Protection Act?
2. What sanctions would you introduce for breaches of the law on data protection?

3. What do you understand by:
   (a) privacy
   (b) confidentiality
   (c) anonymity?
   Illustrate your answer with examples drawn from social research.

☐ Statements of Ethical Practice

Many learned societies have devised principles of ethical practice to indicate some of the major problems that their members may confront when conducting social research. Some learned societies have rules that are actively enforced, while others, such as the British Sociological Association (BSA), provide a framework within which it is suggested researchers should work. This reading provides some sections of the BSA Statement.

Reading 5

Styles of sociological work are diverse and subject to change, not least because sociologists work within a wide variety of settings. Sociologists, in carrying out their work, inevitably face ethical, and sometimes legal, dilemmas which arise out of competing obligations and conflicts of interest. The following statement aims to alert members of the Association to issues that raise ethical concerns and to indicate potential problems and conflicts of interest that might arise in the course of their professional activities.

While they are not exhaustive, the statement points to a set of obligations to which members should normally adhere as principles for guiding their conduct. Departures from the principles should be the result of deliberation and not ignorance. The strength of this statement and its binding force rest ultimately on active discussion, reflection and continued use by sociologists. In addition, the statement will help to communicate the professional position of sociologists to others, especially those involved in or affected by the activities of sociologists.

The statement is meant, primarily, to inform members' ethical judgements rather than to impose on them an external set of standards. The purpose is to make members aware of the ethical issues that may arise in their work, and to encourage them to educate themselves and their colleagues to behave ethically. The statement does not, therefore, provide a set of recipes for resolving ethical choices or dilemmas, but recognises that often it will be necessary to make such choices on the basis of principles and values, and the interests of those involved.

Sociologists, when they carry out research, enter into personal and moral relationships with those they study, be they individuals, households, social groups or corporate entities. Although sociologists, like other researchers are committed to the advancement of knowledge, that goal does not, of itself, provide an entitlement to override the rights of others. Members must satisfy themselves that a study is necessary for the furtherance of knowledge before embarking upon it. Members should be aware that they have some responsibility for the use to which their research may be put. Discharging that responsibility may on occasion be difficult, especially in situations of social conflict, competing social interests or where there is unanticipated misuse of the research by third parties.

Relationships with research participants

(a) Sociologists have a responsibility to ensure that the physical, social and psychological well-being of research participants is not adversely affected by research. They should strive to protect the rights of those they study, their interests, sensitivities and privacy, while recognising the difficulty of balancing potentially conflicting interests. Because sociologists study the relatively powerless as well as those more powerful than themselves, research relationships are frequently characterised by disparities of power and status. Despite this, research relationships should be characterised, whenever possible, by trust. In some cases, where the public interest dictates otherwise and particularly where power is being abused, obligations of trust and protection may weigh less heavily. Nevertheless, these obligations should not be discarded lightly.

(b) As far as possible sociological research should be based on the freely given informed consent of those studied. This implies a responsibility on the sociologist to explain as fully as possible, and in terms meaningful to participants, what the research is about, who is undertaking and financing it, why it is being undertaken and how it is to be promoted.

   (i) Research participants should be aware of their right to refuse participation whenever and for whatever reason they wish. They should also not be under the impression that they are required to participate.

   (ii) Research participants should understand how far they will be afforded anonymity and confidentiality and should be able to reject the use of data-gathering devices such as tape-recorders and video cameras.

(iii) Where there is a likelihood that data may be shared with other researchers, the potetial uses to which the data might be put may need to be discussed with research participants.

(iv) When filming or recording for research purposes, sociologists should make clear to research participants the purpose of the filming or recording, and, as precisely as possible, to whom it will be communicated. Sociologists should be careful, on the one hand, not to give unrealistic guarantees of confidentiality and, on the other, not to permit communication of research films or records to audiences other than those to which research participants have agreed.

(v) It should also be borne in mind that in some research contexts, especially those involving field research, it may be necessary for the obtaining of consent to be regarded, not as a once-and-for-all prior event, but as a process, subject to renegotation over time. In addition, particular care may need to be taken during periods of prolonged fieldwork where it is easy for research participants to forget that they are being studied.

(vi) In some situations access to a research setting is gained via a 'gatekeeper'. In these situations members should adhere to the principle of obtaining informed consent directly from research participants to whom access is required, while at the same time taking account of the gatekeeper's interest. Since the relationship between research participants and the gatekeeper will continue long after the sociologist has left the research setting, care should be taken not to inadvertently disturb that relationship unduly.

(c) It is incumbent upon members to be aware of the possible consequences of their work. Wherever possible they should attempt to anticipate, and to guard against, consequences for research participants which can be predicted to be harmful. Members are not absolved from this responsibility by the consent given by research participants.

(d) In many of its guises, social research intrudes into the lives of those studied. While some participants in sociological research may find the experience a positive and welcome one, for others the experience may be disturbing. Even if not exposed to harm, those studied may feel wronged by aspects of the research process. This can be particularly so if they perceive apparent intrusions into their private and personal worlds, or where research gives rise to false hopes, uncalled-for self-knowledge, or unnecessary anxiety. Members should consider carefully the possibility that the research experience may be a disturbing one and, normally, should attempt to minimize disturbance to those participating in research. It should be borne in mind that decisions made on the basis of research may have effects on individuals as members of a group, even if individual research participants are protected by confidentiality and anonymity.

(e) Special care should be taken where research participants are particularly vulnerable by virtue of factors such as age, social status and powerlessness. Where research participants are ill or too young or too old to participate, proxies may need to be used in order to gather data. In these situations care should be taken not to intrude on the personal space of the person to whom the data ultimately refer, or to disturb the relationship between this person and the proxy. Where it can be inferred that the person about whom data are sought would object to supplying certain kinds of information, that material should not be sought from the proxy.

British Sociological Association (1992), 'Statement of Ethical Practice', *Sociology*, Vol. 26, No. 4, pp. 703–4, 705.

Questions

1. What do you understand to be the purpose of a Statement of Ethical Principles? How does it differ from rules?
2. How would you explain to research participants what their rights are?
3. Who would you consider to be 'vulnerable research participants' and how would you take 'special care' in working with them?

☐ Informed Consent

Many statements of ethical principles focus on informed consent – an idea developed within the Nuremberg Code (following World War Two) which discussed the voluntary consent of human subjects. In this reading, I provide examples of informed consent from my study of a comprehensive school.

Reading 6

On gaining access to teacher job interviews I reached an agreement with the head whereby he would either introduce me to all candidates or he would give me an opening to do this for myself. However, I soon found that this rarely happened in a systematic way. In the first job interviews that I sat in on the head gave me the opportunity to introduce myself to candidates and to ask if they had any objections to me being present. Needless to say, neither of the candidates indicated any objection nor for that matter have any candidates since. However, it is dubious whether this kind of situation can be regarded as constituting informed consent given the power relations involved in the situation. What candidate would risk having me ejected from an interview when it was apparent that the head and the governors had invited me into the situation?

However, there were also situations where I was not given an opportunity to introduce myself nor did the head provide any introduction. Then there were other occasions when the head met all candidates who were on interview for a post. Here, I was introduced in the following way:

> This is Mr Burgess from Warwick University. He's doing some research with us and will be sat in the interviews. He's a sort of 'fly on the wall'.

While this statement might have satisfied the head, it could hardly be regarded as informed consent. Indeed, a teacher who subsequently came to McGregor School told me that when I had been introduced in this way there had been speculation among the candidates as to what I was really doing. In a similar way, local authority advisers who sat in on interviews were rarely any better informed. As McGregor is a Catholic school they were present as the guests of the governing body. Often different advisers arrived to conduct interviews. On several occasions they were late and unless specifically asked there was no opportunity to introduce myself or my project unless it was specifically raised by the head or by a governor during an interlude. On this basis, it could be argued that data collection took place under different conditions concerning the relative 'openness' of my research activity. However, it is not possible within such formal situations to make an announcement about research activity prior to each interview. Nevertheless, my research activities could not be regarded as covert to those people involved in interviews as I sat with notebook and pen and openly made notes throughout each interview session. As a consequence the topic of my research or as the chairman of governors called it, my 'minute taking', became a topic of conversation which made it very public to all concerned. But it was doubtful whether all of the people in the interviews had a similar understanding of the research.

My problems did not end there. Part of my agreement about sitting in on job interviews related to my own activities. I agreed that I would not take any part in the proceedings nor would I divulge any information to teachers about what transpired in the interviews. However, I soon found that this was far from straightforward. When the first group of informal interviews occurred for a post I joined the head. All went well until lunchtime when we were joined by a governor. The governor began by asking the head to rank the candidates that we had seen in order of preference for the formal interviews in the afternoon. Once the head had responded the governor turned to me 'And what do you think?' he asked. I explained that I was not there to pass comments on the candidates. 'But I'm interested in what you think' he said. I still persisted, saying that I was not there to make judgments, but he taunted me with the comment 'Why don't you think?' At this point I remarked that I had a moral position to keep up to which the governor replied: 'I'm not worried about your moral position'. Clearly, it was not going to be easy to be 'a fly on the wall'. In subsequent interviews I was asked questions by governors about candidates and about references. Usually, I tried to deflect these questions by means of a non-committal response so that I would not directly influence the decisions that were made. However, I did break with this convention on one occasion when in the middle of meeting candidates and interviewing them one governor turned and asked me what the post was about for which they were interviewing. It was the kind of question that was unexpected but I felt obliged to address it.

R.G. Burgess (1989), 'Grey Areas: ethical dilemmas in educational ethnography' In R.G. Burgess (ed), *The Ethics of Educational Research*, pp. 65–6.

Questions

1. What do you understand by 'informed consent'?
2. In what ways was informed consent problematic in my study?
3. Did my research raise issues of overt and covert study? Give reasons for your answer.

Project Questions

1. Design a statement of ethical principles for students doing small-scale research projects.
2. Consider the circumstances in which covert research would need to be conducted. Outline the problems that would arise for you as a researcher.
3. What ethical problems need to be considered when disseminating data?

Further Reading

While there are now many books concerned with ethical issues in social research it is also important to reflect on the ethical issues involved in empirical studies that you have read.

J.A. Barnes, *Who Should Know What? Social Science, Privacy and Ethics* (Penguin, 1979), is still the most comprehensive coverage of ethical issues.

S. Bok, *Lying* (Quartet, 1978), is a useful guide to the complex circumstances surrounding truth telling and lying.

British Sociological Association, *Statement of Ethical Practice* (1992), provides an outline of professional practice in relation to ethical dilemmas. It is contained in the journal *Sociology*, Vol. 26, No. 4, 1992, pp. 703–7.

M. Bulmer (ed), *Social Research Ethics* (Macmillan, 1982), is mainly concerned with the overt–covert debate.

R.G. Burgess (ed), *The Ethics of Educational Research* (Falmer Press, 1989), contains essays on the ethical problems that arise in a range of projects using surveys, statistics, ethnography, feminist methods and so on.

Among the empirical studies that can be considered for the ethical dilemmas faced by the researcher are:

R.G. Burgess, *Experiencing Comprehensive Education: A Study of Bishop McGregor School* (Methuen, 1983).

R. Cavendish, *Women on the Line* (Routledge, 1982).

M. Mac an Ghaill, *Young, Gifted and Black* (Open University Press, 1990).

W.F. Whyte, *Street Corner Society* (University of Chicago Press, 1981).

10 Analysing data and writing about research

Many of the books that focus on research methods highlight the importance of techniques of social investigation. While this book has put research methods in the spotlight, it has taken the opportunity to discuss their relationship with the research process. Accordingly, throughout this volume research methods have been examined in relation to research design, data collection and, in part, data analysis. In this chapter, we focus on the links between research methods and data analysis before turning to the implications for theorising, publishing and disseminating data.

All researchers have to consider whether they are going to utilise primary data which involves collecting and analysing them personally or secondary data which involves the researcher in utilising data that have been collected by others. This decision is particularly relevant for those who wish to conduct large-scale investigations. Social researchers who decide to collect their own data in such studies may use survey instruments to collect the data, but having assembled the data, decisions have to be taken about the way in which they are to be coded (see Chapter 5) and, in turn, the kinds of tables that are to be derived from the analysis. Many of these issues need to be considered before the study begins so that there is a good link between the design, collection and analysis of data.

Another way in which researchers may obtain access to large-scale studies and their data is through secondary data analysis. The best known large-scale survey that is conducted in the United Kingdom every ten years is the Census which includes questions about age, sex, members of households and accommodation, among other topics, for the whole of the population. It is possible to get access to the statistical evidence for the area in which you live by using the Small Area Statistics.

A further survey that can be used for secondary data analysis is the General Household Survey (GHS). This is a continuous survey which was started by the Office of Population Censuses and Surveys in 1971. It contains data relating to a sample of the population on a range of topics including: work, health and education. Whenever you consider conducting a survey, it is worth looking at the General Household Survey so that you can decide whether to ask similar questions in order to compare data sets. In asking questions about education, the GHS has covered such topics as: type of school, college and so on that the individual has attended, terminal education age, qualifications, current education and apprenticeships, and the respondent's father's occupation. In recent years, topics have been added including: teacher training, nursery schooling and recreational classes. Overall, this survey, together with many others conducted by government departments, contain data that provide useful material for the social researcher.

There are also some national cohorts or longitudinal studies that contain data for subsequent analysis and use by other researchers. Among the best known are the studies conducted by J.W.B. Douglas which resulted in important insights on education in his book *The Home and the School* (1964). Similarly, the longitudinal study conducted by the National Children's Bureau on the physical, social and educational development of 16,000 children born in the first week of March 1958 (see Fogelman 1983), is available for further analysis. In short, researchers have many studies that can be used for the purpose of secondary data analysis of large-scale data sets.

However, those researchers who wish to focus on small-scale situations need to analyse observational material contained in field notes, interview transcripts and documentary evidence. Here, analysis is not a separate stage of the investigation but occurs simultaneously with data collection. Many researchers have pointed to the importance of reading and rereading field notes in order to focus on their studies, develop themes and in turn generate theory. Field notes and interview transcripts need to be carefully coded, referenced and arranged according to topics and conceptual categories that can be used in the final report.

A key question for researchers using qualitative data has been summarised by Lofland who suggests they should ask:

> What are the characteristics of acts, activities, meanings, participation, relationships, and settings, the forms they assume, the variations they display?
>
> *(Lofland, 1971, p. 15)*

By using this question, Lofland suggests some of the main units of study that can be used in qualitative analysis which may contribute to the description of social phenomena and also the generation of concepts and theories about the social situation that is studied.

Such accounts are provided in papers presented at conferences, in articles published in academic journals and in books. But the responsibility of the researcher does not end at this point. Many studies raise questions about the social, ethical and political context in which reporting occurs. Accordingly, researchers need to consider a range of questions about their data and the reports that are made public including:

- Who owns the data?
- In what form should data be made public?
- In what form should researchers publish their data?
- What can be done to minimise harm to individuals and groups?

Accordingly, this brings us back to the issues that several researchers have raised about the ethical principles adopted by the research community. In turn, it also raises questions about the way in which research data can be evaluated and used. In this respect, when writing and reading accounts of research, the following issues should be considered:

1 How the research began, including who sponsored it and the key questions raised.
2 What methods of data collection were used and what kinds of data were provided.
3 Whether the data are reliable and valid.
4 The way in which data are presented and used.
5 The implications of the research for theory, policy and practice.

All these issues are important when using research methods and need careful consideration in conducting social research and evaluating studies conducted by other researchers.

☐ Analysing Survey Data

Survey data analysis is part of the research process which begins with the coding of questionnaires and continues with ways in which variables can be prepared. The analysis clarifies initial relationships and accounts for the findings. In this reading, Bryan Glastonbury and Jill MacKean discuss the practicalities of survey analysis.

Reading 1

If you are planning to collect quantitative data on more than a very few individuals, it is sensible to use a computer to analyze the results. Anyone who has tried to sort out and analyze the results of a survey without the help of a computer will know that, even with a small amount of data, the job is formidable. It is perfectly *possible* to do simple analyses either by sorting questionnaires (or forms) by the answers to a particular question, and counting the various piles or by writing all the responses on to large pieces of paper. Many people who have not used a computer before feel that it would take longer to learn how to use one than it would take to do the analysis 'by hand' – and many people have realized that this was a mistake! There are several good reasons why it is advisable to use a computer to analyze data of this kind. Obviously if the number of cases is very small and the analyses required are very simple, then a simple hand-counting method might be as quick. But usually the time taken to learn the necessary basics is time well spent. For one thing you will have learnt a new skill which might very well be useful to you later on. Another reason for using a computer is that once you have the data in computer-readable form you can do as many analyses as you want to merely by using a few keys on the keyboard. It might be that you start off with the idea that it is really only a few tables that you want, but having considered these tables you realize that further and more complex statistical analyses are needed. If you have not prepared your data for the computer you might have an almost impossible task trying to do it by hand. You might then have to use the computer after all! Any analysis that involves multivariate techniques (where more than one variable is considered at a time) is much better done on a computer, not only because of the time saved but because a computer is less liable to make mistakes.

It is important to know exactly how you are going to handle and analyze your data before you start to collect it. Your questionnaire should be designed in such a way that it is simple to key most of the information directly into the computer. You must decide how you will handle multiple response variables (those variables where you may want to record more than one value from an answer) and variables that need coding after they have been returned to you. A code book (or dictionary) must be created. The minimum information to be included will generally include the variable name, variable values, value labels, the codes to be given missing values and the maximum number of characters that the variable can take.

After the code book is written and the questionnaires checked and coded, the data is ready for input. There are various methods that can be used. A wordprocessor or editor can be used and the data saved as an ASCII (American Standard Code for Information Interchange) file which can be used by other computer packages. It is sensible to decide which package you are going to use for the analysis, as different packages require the data laid out in different ways. Fixed format is a generally accepted method – each case starts on a new line and can continue for as many lines as necessary, and each variable occupies the same column or columns for each case.

Alternatively a spreadsheet package (e.g. Lotus 123) or a database package (e.g. dBase III) can be used. These can store not only data but some data description, such as variable names, as well. They cannot produce much in the way of analysis (although Lotus 123 can produce graphics) but they can write files which can be read by other analysis packages.

Another option is to use a data-entry package such as SPSS-PC Data Entry. With this package a framework is set up containing the data description into which the data is punched. Various edits can be imposed, such as 'ranges' which only allow certain values to be punched in and 'rules' which do not allow specified inconsistency (such as someone who has an age keyed in as 5 to have three children). Another useful facility is 'Skip and Fill'. If there are some parts of the form or questionnaire which do not apply to everyone, then you might want to fill all these variables with some missing value (such as 99) and go to the next relevant variable. This can save a lot of time. Data can be entered in the form of a spreadsheet with the variable names appearing at the top of the columns or, alternatively, a form can be designed which can be set up to look like the original questionnaire (or to take any format desired). The data and the data description can be saved together for later analysis by SPSS. ASCII files can be written out to be used by other packages. The package is menu-driven and easy to use.

The software package chosen will depend on availability and the type of analysis required. There are many packages available and a few of the most useful will be briefly mentioned. Most have mainframe and personal computer (PC) versions.

So, which to choose? It will depend on the number of cases that you have, the sort of data sets and what you want to do. If you have a small number of cases, a simple data set and want simple analyses then MINITAB might be suitable as it is so easy to use, but it is very limited. SNAP also has limitations on size (a tendency with many PC programs or PC versions where there is limited storage space on the computer), but is rather more versatile. For a larger more complex data set or for more complex analyses, SPSS, BMDP or SAS would be more suitable. It is important to decide which package you are going to use at an early stage in your project. You should have thought about what sort of analysis you want to carry out and you can consult the manuals or seek advice to see which package is most suitable for your purpose. You need to think about the analysis before you collect the data. Very often it is left until all the data has been collected which makes things much more difficult.

B. Glastonbury and J. MacKean (1991), 'Survey Methods' in G. Allen and C. Skinner (eds), *Handbook for Research Students in the Social Sciences*, pp. 243–6.

Questions

1. What are the advantages of using a computer to analyse data?
2. In what ways can survey data be prepared for data analysis?
3. What is the relationship between survey design, data collection and data analysis? What issues need to be addressed to avoid difficulties with analysis?

☐ Secondary Data Analysis

Within the social science literature distinctions are made between 'primary research', where the investigator collects the data, and 'secondary analysis', where the investigator uses the data that has been collected by other people. In this reading, Michael Procter examines the advantages and disadvantages of secondary analysis.

Reading 2

It may be helpful to summarise here the advantages and limitations of secondary analysis, even though many of these points will also be made later. As you might expect, the overall conclusion is in favour of this methodology, but a number of warnings are offered.

Surely the most obvious advantage of secondary analysis is **cost**. For many researchers there is no possibility of obtaining funding at the level required for survey work.

In addition, it is argued, a great deal of **time** can be saved. First, if the data already exist, then new analysts can get to work almost as soon as they think of the idea, instead of having to face years of preparation and fieldwork if they are to be responsible for their own data collection. Second, if one is primarily employed as a teacher, as most academic researchers are, one may never be able to find the time to run one's own project from start to finish – unless one can cut out a whole section of the work by starting at the point where the data have been collected. Similar considerations apply to student researchers, who have, in addition, externally imposed deadlines to cope with.

On the other hand, it cannot be denied that a rather rosy picture has just been painted. The process of obtaining the data and knocking them into shape on one's own computer can take many months and, though this is unlikely ever to approach the time needed to carry out a substantial survey in the field, it can still sometimes be more time than is allowed by, for instance, an undergraduate dissertation deadline. Probably the best advice is not to commit oneself to this form of research without first discussing its pitfalls with a more experienced adviser.

At its best, the **quality** of data obtained in this way is likely to be higher than a relatively inexperienced researcher can hope to obtain unaided. Government survey organisations, in particular, have great expertise in their chosen method, and because their clients are usually government departments they can often bring to bear the political pressure that is needed to legitimise the relatively expensive technology they employ: nationally representative probability samples, highly trained and closely supervised interviewers, the necessary sequence of pilot studies, etc.

On the other hand, all this technical excellence is completely beside the point if the questions asked are not relevant to your research problem. There is always a temptation for the subject of research to be determined by what is convenient rather than by what is scientifically important, and the balance of effort between data collection and data analysis makes this particularly dangerous in planning secondary analysis. 🐦

Widely used data sets often receive special support from the agency through which they are made available. For instance, in the United Kingdom the Economic and Social Research Council (ESRC) Data Archive runs a variety of 'data use' workshops for people working on material such as the General Household Survey and the National Child Development Study. These can be wonderful opportunities for lone researchers to get the intellectual support they need, and especially for beginners to benefit from the often uncodified wisdom of more experienced workers.

Even though the original purpose of a survey may not have been connected with the particular subgroup you wish to focus on, sample sizes are often so large that otherwise **inaccessible populations** can be reached, especially if it is legitimate to merge successive years' samples. For instance, Hornsby-Smith and Dale (1988) were able to study recent Irish immigrants to the United

Kingdom in this way. To collect their own data, they would first have had to obtain a list from which to sample, a substantial project in itself.

However, there can be pitfalls in the **sample design**, into which one would be unlikely to fall in planning the project from scratch. To cite a classic example, the UK Family Expenditure Survey, which is a survey of private households and thus excludes people living in pubs and bars, has proved to be entirely inappropriate as a source of information about alcohol consumption.

It is often unrealistic for a researcher, especially a relatively junior one, to plan to collect data over a period of years, if only because one's career requires that one 'publish or perish' over a relatively short **time span**. And yet data collected over an extended period of time is often precisely what is required by the logic of the research problem. For instance, a cross-sectional analysis (in which all the data are collected at one point in time) shows that heavy drinkers are healthier than light drinkers and teetotallers. To some extent the relationship can be clarified (using the approach outlined in the previous chapter) by showing that drinking generally declines with age, for the most part, because of life cycle changes, and that of course older people tend to be less healthy. However, until we follow the same individuals through time we fail to realise that reduction in drinking often follows and, presumably, is a result of declining health rather than preceding and causing it.

The solution may be to make use of an existing **longitudinal** data set, so that the waiting period has already taken place when the researcher gets to work.

● Social researchers have long been concerned about a variety of **ethical issues** raised by their research. Many of these issues are concerned with the intrusive nature of research on individuals. Secondary analysts might therefore think that, since they are not directly involved in data collection, they are exempt from such concerns. This is not so. There is not sufficient space here to attempt a full discussion of the ethical problems faced in secondary analysis (see Dale et al., 1988), but mention should be made of the continued need for maintaining anonymity – perhaps even more important than in the primary analysis, because the respondents are not in general aware of the uses to which their answers will be put in subsequent work. In practice responsible researchers will ensure anonymity when depositing their data at the data archive, and secondary analysts will have the necessary restrictions imposed on them, but they should remain aware of their responsibilities in this respect.

M. Procter (1993), 'Analysing Other Researchers' Data' in N. Gilbert (ed), *Researching Social Life*, pp. 256–8.

Questions

1. Evaluate the advantages and disadvantages that Michael Procter gives for using secondary data analysis.
2. List some of the main data sets that you can use to conduct secondary analysis. Suggest ways in which these data sets can be used.
3. What ethical issues do you think are involved in secondary data analysis?

☐ Sorting and Organising Qualitative Data

Researchers who engage in qualitative data collection soon find that they accumulate large quantities of data through field notes, interview transcripts, personal diaries and other documentary material. A key task is to work out an effective way to code, sort and organise these data. Many computer programs (such as Ethnograph, Qualpro and Text Analysis) are now available to help the researcher but the main principles of coding and sorting remain. The computer can help to speed up the work.

Reading 3

Becker's advice in those pre-processor days was to put important bits of data (quotes from an informant, an observation, a vignette, an insight recorded during notetaking) on individual 3 x 5 or 5 x 8 cards, or half-sheets of typing paper. The sorting was literal: You sat at a table (or on the floor) and physically divided up your great bundle of data "cards" by putting them into smaller piles according to categories that allowed you a first run at organizing your material. The big technological breakthrough of the day was the key-sort punch card, an index card ringed with holes on all sides that could be punched open according to whatever coding system the researcher devised. With your cards lined up in front of you, each containing some discrete bit of data and code-punched around the edges, you had only to insert one or more rods through the stack of cards and then shake them. Your coding and punching system enabled the rods to separate the cards you wanted from the others.

Some researchers continue to use coding systems based on that punch-card principle. I don't, because when I might have used them I couldn't afford them, and I grew accustomed to putting data on 5 x 8 papers easily typed or handwritten, easily stored, and easily sorted. My little stacks of cards or papers may seem archaic in a computer age, but I describe them to help others visualize processes partially hidden by modern technology. I marvel at software programs like THE ETHNOGRAPH, QUAL-PRO, or TEXT ANALYSIS PACKAGE (TAP) designed for data management with personal computers. Keep in mind, however, that most programs are attuned better to the almost limitless capacities of microcomputers than to the finite capacities of human researchers. In THE ETHNOGRAPH, for example, a "line" of text – ranging from a single word to an entire interview – can be coded into as many as seven different categories. This is a great convenience once one has arrived at the categorizing stage. But for anyone having trouble *sorting* data, a program that allowed initially for no more than two or three categories might prove a blessing rather than a needless constraint.

I repeat: The critical task in qualitative research is not to accumulate all the data you can, but to "can" (i.e., get rid of) most of the data you accumulate. This requires constant winnowing. The trick is to discover essences and then to reveal those essences with sufficient context, yet not become mired trying to include everything that might possibly be described. Audiotapes, videotapes, and now computer capabilities entreat us to do just the opposite; they have gargantuan appetites *and* stomachs. Because we can accommodate ever-increasing quantities of data – mountains of it – we have to be careful not to get buried by avalanches of our own making.

This problem of data overload has a parallel in one of the unanticipated consequences of the copy machines now so readily available in our libraries. In my student days, when we were given reading assignments, we went to the library and read the material, typically distilling the key ideas and copying a few telling quotes onto reading cards. Today's students copy entire articles and books intact. Their visits to the library are more efficient than ours were, except in one important way: When they leave, they have not begun the assignment. When they do get around to their reading, they probably will underline or highlight huge passages of text with a felt pen, rather than identify key phrases and summarize the rest in their own words. This is not good training for descriptive research. The parallel style in fieldwork is referred to disparagingly as the vacuum-cleaner approach, in which fieldworkers attempt to see and record *everything*. There is a division between those qualitative researchers who want to impress upon students how *much* they can observe and those who place the emphasis on how *well*.

H.F. Wolcott (1990), *Writing Up Qualitative Research*, pp. 34–5.

Questions

1. List the important 'bits' of qualitative data that you need to consider for data analysis. Give reasons why each of the 'bits' you mention is important.
2. Harry Wolcott argues that the critical task in qualitative research is not to accumulate data but to get rid of it. Do you agree? If so, why? If not, why not?
3. Suggest ways in which you can overcome a 'vacuum cleaner' approach to doing fieldwork.

☐ Developing a Formal Theory

Although there has been much discussion about the importance of developing theory in the course of conducting research, there is relatively little direction given about how this can be done. In this reading, Anselm Strauss summarises the key steps involved in the development of formal theory.

Reading 4

1. Choose a phenomenon, and give it a name, for this will be your core category, to which all your codes will relate.
2. Select and examine some data in which your phenomenon, named as the core category, appears. This data may be drawn from an interview, fieldnote, newspaper account, article in a popular magazine, paper in a technical magazine, novel – in fact, any document – or from your own or someone else's experience.
3. Begin to code these data in the usual fashion: dimensions, subcategories, etc., and in accordance with the coding paradigm.
4. Begin to write theoretical memos incorporating your initial ideas and the results of your coding.
5. Employ theoretical sampling, seeking your next data in a different substantive area. This will yield new subcategories and begin to give variance to the previous analyses.
6. Continue to do that, theoretically sampling within the same substantive areas but also in widely differing ones. This tends to greatly extend the similarities and differences brought into the analysis, while continuing to densify the analysis itself.
7. At every step of the analysis, think comparatively – not merely to suggest new theoretical samples (sources,

events, actors, organizations, processes) but to enrich your specific codes and theoretical memos.

8. As you do all this, you will both notice the usual develop- ment of conceptual density and find yourself, almost from the outset, not merely doing open coding but beginning to do selective coding. This is because you will be relating subcategories to the core category under study. So the final rule of thumb illustrated in this chapter is: Be very aware of how all codes that you develop bear on the core phenomenon, and make the connections as *specific as possible.*

A.L. Strauss (1987), *Qualitative Analysis for Social Scientists*, pp. 241–2.

Questions

1. Briefly summarise in your own words what you understand to be the key steps in developing formal theory.
2. Choose a social phenomenon that is in the news. Collect newspaper accounts and magazine articles on the phenomenon and attempt to code the data in these articles. What are the difficulties involved and how can they be resolved?
3. In relation to the social phenomenon you selected:
   (a) attempt to write a theoretical memo based on the codes you devel- oped which indicates links between codes;
   (b) consider the comparisons you can make to develop your codes, your memos and your concepts.

☐ Problems of Publishing Research

Once studies are published they are often surrounded by discus- sion and debate among a variety of people including those who were originally studied. A classic example from America is the Springdale case where researchers wrote a book entitled *Small Town in Mass Society*. The book resulted in a range of objections. In this reading, the editors of the journal *Human Organisation* highlight some of the issues.

Reading 5

A small upstate New York village has now been immortalized in anthropological literature under the name of "Springdale." The local newspaper reports that the experience has not been entirely a pleasing one. We pass on this account:

"The people of the Village [Springdale] waited quite awhile to get even with Art Vidich, who wrote a *Peyton Place*-type book about their town recently.

"The featured float of the annual Fourth of July parade followed an authentic copy of the jacket of the book, *Small Town in Mass Society*, done large-scale by Mrs. Beverly Robinson. Following the book cover came residents of [Springdale] riding masked in cars labeled with the fictitious names given them in the book.

"But the pay-off was the final scene, a manure-spreader filled with very rich barnyard fertilizer, over which was bending an effigy of 'The Author.' "

The account suggests that a good time was had by all – on this particular occasion. Nevertheless, local observers report that the disturbance caused by the book in the village has not been entirely compensated for by even such a ceremony carried out in the best anthropological traditions. The book and its aftermath raise some serious questions.

'Editorial-Freedom and Responsibility in Research: The "Springdale" Case' in *Human Organisation*, Vol. 17 (1958–9), p. 1.

Questions

1. Using the quotation from the newspaper article, suggest reasons why the book *Small Town in Mass Society* was controversial.
2. If individuals are identified in a study, can anything be done to avoid damage to them?
3. Consider any study with which you are familiar and discuss the questions that are raised by the material published. (The topics you consider may relate to publication and the ways in which published data could be used.)

□ Research Dissemination and the Media

Local and national newspapers often carry brief accounts about research. While this has the advantage of conveying information, it is not always accurate. I am conducting a study entitled 'Teaching and Learning About Food and Nutrition in Schools'. The project has been reported in the press in different ways as shown in the three accounts provided in this reading.

Reading 6

A reporter from *The Birmingham Post* conducted an interview with me, and the following article appeared:

Professor in search for pupils with taste
By DOROTHY LEPKOWSKA
Education Correspondent

School dinners are to be scrutinised as part of a nationwide study into children's eating habits.

Prof Robert Burgess, a professor of sociology at Warwick University, will spend two years visiting schools, where he will also look at the role they play in children's knowledge of nutrition.

The study is part of a £1.4 million six-year project which will be the first of its kind to look into the eating habits of children in Britain.

It is being paid for by the government's Economic and Social Research Council.

Yesterday Prof Burgess said he was entering his research with a completely open mind.

He said: "Adults always think children eat what isn't good for them, but I will be seeking to find out whether that is the case.

"I will be particularly interested to look into the McDonald's culture which somehow sits alongside the healthy eating ethos schools are attempting to transmit."

"We will be asking children to keep diaries of what they eat throughout the day to find out how far they are influenced by what they eat at school, and at home."

Experts will sit in on classes where food nutrition is being discussed and will attend special events, such as Food Weeks, organised by schools.

Pupils at four Midland schools – two primary and two secondary – will be investigated in depth, but Prof Burgess declined to say which ones.

"They will be situated in different socio-economic areas so we get a good cross-section of population and identify how culture influences what people eat," he said.

"If children chose to spend their lunch money in the local chip shop instead of in the school canteen then we will follow them to find out what they buy."

The Birmingham Post, 25th August 1992.

The Birmingham Evening Mail did not contact me but printed this account:

Expert probes school dinners

A Midland academic is joining a nationwide study into children's eating habits by scrutinising school dinners.

Prof Robert Burgess, a professor of sociology at Warwick University, will spend two years visiting schools, to look at the role they play in children's knowledge of nutrition.

Project

The study is part of a project funded by the government's Economic and Social Research Council, the first of its kind to look into the eating habits of children in Britain.

Prof Burgess said: "Adults always think children eat what isn't good for them but I will be seeking to find out whether that is the case.

"I will be particularly interested to look into the McDonald's culture which somehow sits alongside the healthy eating ethos schools are attempting to transmit."

The Birmingham Evening Mail, 25th August 1992.

The Sun did not conduct any interview with me but printed the following article:

Din-dins prof hunts chip kids

A professor is to share bags of chips with kids for two years – to find out why they prefer junk food to school dinners.

Sociologist Robert Burgess, dubbed Doctor Din-dins, will visit schools around the country and follow children on lunchtime trips.

The Warwick University professor fears kids are developing a "McDonald's culture."

His survey is part of a six-year national study costing £1.4 million.

The Sun, 26th August 1992.

Questions

1. Given the project title, in what ways do the articles oversimplify the research?
2. Compare the three articles and suggest what you consider to be the key features of the project.
3. What have you learned from these accounts about the use of newspaper articles as research evidence?

Project Questions

1. In relation to a project of your choice, consider the extent to which you can collect
   (a) primary data

(b) secondary data.
2. Using either a set of field notes or an interview transcript, decide on the way in which it can be coded and analysed.
3. Write a press release of not more than 300 words on a project you have conducted. Consider the main issues you wish to communicate.

Further Reading

H. Becker, *Writing for Social Scientists* (University of Chicago Press, 1986), gives some useful guidance on writing strategies.

A. Bryman and R.G. Burgess (eds), *Analysing Qualitative Data* (Routledge, 1994), is a collection of essays in which individuals, teams, ethnographers and case-study workers discuss qualitative analysis.

A. Dale, S. Arber and M. Procter, *Doing Secondary Analysis* (Unwin Hyman, 1988), is an excellent practical guide to secondary analysis.

D.A. de Vaus, *Surveys in Social Research* (Unwin Hyman, 1986), provides a good discussion of survey analysis.

N. Gilbert (ed), *Researching Social Life* (Sage, 1993), contains several useful chapters on data analysis and writing.

C. Haslam and A. Bryman (eds) *Social Scientists Meet the Media* (Routledge, 1994), provides discussions of social scientists' encounters with the media.

L. Richardson, *Writing Strategies* (Sage, 1990), provides an account of writing a book.

M. Stacey, *Methods of Social Research* (Pergamon, 1969), contains a very useful overview of survey research that is suitable for students.

A. Strauss, *Qualitative Analysis for Social Scientists* (Cambridge University Press, 1987), is an advanced discussion that is suitable for teachers.

H. Wolcott, *Writing up Qualitative Research* (Sage, 1990), contains practical advice on handling writing problems.

Bibliography

The following list includes all material that is referred to in the text, but does not repeat items that are only listed in the suggestions for further reading at the end of each chapter.

I.K. Birkstead, 'School Performance Viewed from the Boys', *Sociological Review*, vol. 24, 1976, pp. 63–78.

R. Bucher, 'Social Process and Power in a Medical School' in M.N. Zald (ed), *Power in Organisations* (Nashville, Vanderbilt University Press, 1970).

M. Bulmer (ed), *Sociological Research Methods: An Introduction* (London: Macmillan, 1984; 2nd edition).

R.G. Burgess (ed), *Field Research: A Sourcebook and Field Manual* (London: Allen and Unwin, 1982).

R.G. Burgess, *Experiencing Comprehensive Education: A Study of Bishop McGregor School* (London: Methuen, 1983).

R.G. Burgess, *In The Field: An Introduction to Field Research* (London: Allen and Unwin, 1984).

R.G. Burgess (ed), *Strategies of Educational Research: Qualitative Methods* (Lewes: Falmer Press, 1985).

R.G. Burgess (ed), *The Ethics of Educational Research* (Lewes: Falmer Press, 1989).

R.G. Burgess (ed), *Learning About Fieldwork* (London: JAI Press, 1992)

K. Cameron, M.V. Kim and D.A. Whettan, 'Organisational Effects of Decline and Turbulence', *Administrative Science Quarterly*, Vol. 32, No. 2, 1987, pp. 222–40.

D.T. Campbell and D.W. Fiske, 'Convergent and Discriminant Validation by the Multitrait-Multimethod Matrix', *Psychological Bulletin*, Vol. 56, 1959, pp. 81–105.

L. Chisholm, A. Heath and D. Woodward, 'Methodological Problems of Quantitative and Qualitative Research: the national survey of 1960 graduates', *Angewandte Sozialforschung*, Vol. 5, No. 1, 1977, pp. 195–208.

A.V. Cicourel, *Method and Measurement in Sociology* (New York: Free Press, 1964).

A. Dale, S. Arber and M. Procter, *Doing Secondary Analysis* (London: Unwin Hyman, 1988).

N. Denzin, *The Research Act* (Chicago: Aldine, 1970).

D.A. de Vaus, *Surveys in Social Research* (London: Allen and Unwin, 1986).

J.D. Douglas, *The Social Meanings of Suicide* (Princeton, New Jersey: Princeton University Press, 1967).

J.W.B. Douglas, *The Home and the School* (London: Macgibbon and Kee, 1964).

R. Duelli-Klein, 'How We Do What We Want To Do: thoughts about feminist methodology' in G. Bowles and R. Duelli-Klein (eds), *Theories of Women's Studies* (London: Routledge and Kegan Paul, 1983).

K. Fogelman (ed), *Growing Up In Great Britain* (London: Macmillan, 1983).

H.J. Gans, *The Urban Villagers* (New York: Free Press, 1962).

H.J. Gans, *The Levittowners* (London: Allen Lane, 1967)

H. Garfinkel, *Studies in Ethnomethodology* (Englewood Cliffs, New Jersey:

Prentice Hall, 1967).

H.G. Genn and S.B. Burman, 'Report of a Pilot Study of Home Accident Victims' (Oxford: Centre for Socio-Legal Studies Monograph, 1976).

B. Glaser and A. Strauss, *The Discovery of Grounded Theory* (Chicago: Aldine, 1967).

J.H. Goldthorpe *et al.*, *The Affluent Worker: Industrial Attitudes and Behaviour* (Cambridge: Cambridge University Press, 1968).

M. Hammersley and P. Atkinson, *Ethnography: Principles into Practice* (London: Tavistock, 1983).

F.W. Hondius, 'The Work of the Council of Europe in the Area of Data Protection' in Online Conferences Ltd, *Data Regulation: European and Third World Realities* (Uxbridge: Online Conferences Ltd, 1978).

F.W. Hondius, 'The Human Aspects of Data Protection' in J.J.P. Kenny (ed), *Data Privacy and Security: The State of the Art Report* (Oxford: Pergamon Infotech Limited, 1985).

M.P. Hornsby-Smith and A. Dale, 'The Assimilation of Irish Immigrants in England', *British Journal of Sociology*, Vol. 39, No. 4, 1988, pp. 519–44.

G. Huizer, 'The Asocial Role of Social Scientists in Underdeveloped Countries: some ethical considerations', *Sociologies*, Vol. 23, No. 2, 1973, pp. 165–77.

E.D. Ives, *The Tape-Recorded Interview* (Knoxville: University of Tennessee Press, 1974).

D. Locker, *Symptoms and Illness: The Cognitive Organisation of Disorder* (London: Tavistock, 1981).

J. Lofland, *Analysing Social Settings* (Belmont, California: Wadsworth, 1971).

P. Maguire, 'The Psychological and Social Consequences of Breast Cancer', *Nursing Mirror* 140 (14), 1975, pp. 54–7.

M. Mann, 'Socio-Logic', *Sociology*, Vol. 15, No 4, 1981, pp. 544–50.

T. Morris, S. Greer and B. White, 'Psychological and Social Adjustment to Mastectomy – a two year follow up study', *Cancer*, Vol. 40, 1977, pp. 2381–7.

A. Oakley, 'Interviewing Women: A contradiction in terms' in H. Roberts (ed), *Doing Feminist Research* (London: Routledge and Kegan Paul, 1981).

K. Plummer, *Documents of Life* (London: Allen and Unwin, 1983).

N. Polsky, *Hustlers, Beats and Others* (Harmondsworth: Penguin, 1969).

M. Samphier, *A Data Indexing System* (MRC Research Unit, University of Aberdeen, 1976).

R. Samuel (ed), *Village Life and Labour* (London: Routledge and Kegan Paul, 1975)

L. Schatzman and A.L. Strauss, *Field Research: Strategies for a Natural Sociology* (Englewood Cliffs, New Jersey: Prentice Hall, 1973).

H. Simons, 'Conversation Piece: the practice of interviewing in case study research' in C. Adelman (ed), *Uttering Muttering* (London: Grant McIntyre, 1981).

L. Stanley and S. Wise, *Breaking Out: Feminist Consciousness and Feminist Research* (London: Routledge and Kegan Paul, 1983).

W.L. Wallace, *The Logic of Science in Sociology* (Chicago: Aldine, 1971).

R. Wallis, 'The Moral Career of a Research Project' in C. Bell and H. Newby (eds), *Doing Sociological Research* (London: Allen and Unwin, 1977).

J.D. Watson, *The Double Helix* (Harmondsworth: Penguin, 1968).

E.J. Webb *et al.*, *Unobtrusive Measures: Nonreactive Research in the Social Sciences* (Chicago: Rand McNally, 1966).

A. Westin, *Privacy and Freedom* (New York: Atheneeumm, 1967).

M. Zelditch, 'Some Methodological Problems of Field Studies', *American Journal of Sociology*, Vol. 67, No. 5, 1962, pp. 566–76.

Index